HOW TO TAKE ON THE
MEDIA

HOW TO TAKE ON THE

MEDIA

Sarah Dickinson

Weidenfeld and Nicolson
London

To Mr 1% and Fred and Alex

George Weidenfeld and Nicolson Ltd
91 Clapham High Street, London SW4 7TA

ISBN 0 297 82062 1 cased
ISBN 0 297 82018 4 paper

Printed in Great Britain by Butler & Tanner Ltd,
Frome and London

Contents

Contents

PART II   MARRIAGE

Contents

Contents

Preface

Don't get mad, get even.
Senator Everett Dirksen, American politician

The mass media is powerful and pervasive, and you ignore it at your peril. It likes you to be submissive and pliant, and to do as you're told. It often throws in environmental obstacles to make sure you won't try anything as silly as exerting control.

Radio studios tend to go for the 'shabby-chic' look, which invariably undermines self-confidence, and they are usually situated in basements, descending to which provokes an instant mood of gloom. Television force-feeds you with alcohol, shines lights directly into your eyes, and provides seating for anything other than its expected function. Print journalists often move in packs, and brandish notepads and tape-recorders. Their plea of the deadline never fails as a verbal laxative.

As a breed, media people are infused with an overbearing sense of self, revelation of which is concealed by their claim to be 'crusaders for truth'. They are perceptive, sharp and usually good performers. But they are seldom, if ever, as well informed about your subject as you are. They need you as much as you need them. It's ironic that, despite the fact that information is their life-blood, they go so little way towards acknowledging the debt.

As a result, people coming into contact with the media for the first time unconsciously adopt a *reactive* rather than a *proactive* stance. Seldom do they leave an interview having made the points they wanted to make. At best, they are grateful to have 'got through it' with integrity and reputation intact.

Why has this imbalance of power persisted? It's not altogether the fault of the news-gatherers. *You* are just as culpable. If you don't bother to structure your arguments or assert your rights *before* you meet with the media, you mustn't be surprised if you constantly fail to get your points across or to take control. You will also miss opportunities for invaluable free publicity.

How to Take On the Media guides you, step by step, through the media mine-field, breaks down the aura of intimidation, and enables you to communicate with *confidence, clarity and control*.

Sarah Dickinson
June 1990

Acknowledgements

Without WORDPERFECT 5 software, Berol Cardinal HB pencils, Challenge notebooks and my physiotherapist Lizzie Buchanan, it is unlikely that *How to Take on the Media* would have progressed beyond the stage of speculation.

I am also very grateful for the invaluable encouragement and advice given to me by Ed Boyle, 'Dickie' Dickinson, Andrew Hewson, Jim Hiley, Gordon Jones, Graham Lancaster, Dr David Lewis, Iona Salinger, Joan Thirkettle, Nick Williams and my tireless researcher Jacqui Lofthouse, and would like to thank everyone at Ladbroke Radio for their tolerance.

Introduction: The Media

The world continues to offer glittering prizes to those who have stout
hearts and sharp swords.
Frederick Edwin Smith, Earl of Birkenhead, Rectorial address, Glasgow University,
7 November 1923

Britain may no longer be able to lead the field in invention and
manufacturing output, but she rightly retains her reputation
as the most prolific producer of some of the finest quality
newsprint and radio and television programmes in the world.
The collective output is enormous and, with the development
of new technical facilities such as satellite relays and cable TV,
the capacity is still expanding and shows no sign of abating.

At no time in the history of mankind have there been
such breathtaking technological inventions as in our present
century, many of them concerned directly with communications and the birth of the media as we know it today.
We have witnessed the first telephone, the first transmissions
through the ether, with radio broadcasting and receiving, and
the first tentative steps in radar, fostered in the desperation of
war and developed to our present sophisticated TV networks.
Although it's five hundred years since William Caxton built
his first printing press, this century has also seen most of the
developments in the newspaper industry, until it is now able
to gather and disseminate news, literally, at the speed of light.

The whole of this great media industry (radio, press and
television) is sustained and encouraged to further growth by
the public's seemingly insatiable appetite for news, information
and entertainment. The very fact that news and entertainment
in all its forms involves people from all walks of life means that

1

you can become involved at any time, deliberately or by chance, in one or other of the media's domains.

In the following chapters, I will attempt to present the problems, dangers and pitfalls which face the non-professional exposed to the media. Though its outputs are familiar to the reading, listening or viewing public, its methods of operation remain largely esoteric and can be terrifying to the uninitiated who become suddenly exposed to them.

To emerge with success and sanity from a media encounter, you need to be equipped not only with a knowledge of what to expect when first the cameras or microphones are focused upon you, but also with the armaments to enable you to keep calm, whatever the stresses and strains, and to maintain your credibility and conviction throughout your time in the limelight. The opportunity may not often occur, especially if you fail the first time, so it behoves you to be as *well-prepared* as possible before it actually comes to occupying the 'hot seat'.

In order to survive, the media has to appeal to the audience on whom it is largely dependent for its very existence – *you*. It's obliged, therefore, to direct its emphasis and to slant its presentation in the way that will be most popular. You may be dedicated, and without doubt you are master of your subject; you may be the essence of integrity and a paragon of virtue; but your greatest newsworthy attribute may well be the one indiscretion of your life which you would wish above all else to keep out of the proceedings. To paraphrase Mark Antony from Shakespeare's *Julius Caesar*:

> The evil that men do makes good copy, the good is oft interred on the cutting room floor.

The sooner you accept that without you there will be *no* news, and that you or your company is just as likely to be reported as anyone else, the sooner you are going to take a *positive* attitude towards the media and begin taking advantage of what it has to offer. We are talking about *free publicity*:

> 30 seconds on the evening news is worth a front page headline in every newspaper in the world.
> (Edward Guthman, *The Official Rules*, P. Dickson)

Remember that one minute on prime-time television can cost about £100,000.

Television

Thirty-eight million of us watch television for an average of two to three hours every day, and the television news is watched daily by twenty million, often achieving a higher rating than game shows or situation comedies. Rupert Murdoch's Sky Television has the capacity to reach even more viewers, and BSB (British Satellite Broadcasting) promises to extend the audience even further.

At present Britain has four national television networks – BBC 1, BBC 2, ITV and Channel 4, the latter two representing the commercial sector – and a fifth commercial channel and numerous new radio stations are proposed for the early 1990s. The year 1983 saw a revolution in British viewing habits when TV-AM introduced breakfast TV. It quickly adopted an instantly digestible style of pop and pap, whilst its competitor, BBC's *Breakfast Time* (now called *Breakfast News*), valiantly strove for a rather more meaningful presentation of world affairs on the nation's kitchen television screens.

Cable TV is still not nearly as popular in Britain as it is in Europe, but it's estimated that by 1992 five million homes will receive their pictures this way. They will also have the advantage, so the Cable Authority predicts, of being able to tap into many other satellite services, as well as to conduct personal business and shopping transactions without leaving the living room.

Television makes more impact on an audience than all the other media put together. Ironically, its universal appeal has led to most of us treating it with as much regard as running water, only really taking notice if it presents us with something out of the ordinary. And even that can backfire from an essential message. A TV audience will spend time studying a

3

union leader's hair style rather than concentrating on what he's saying.

Try an experiment. Carefully watch a news bulletin, mentally noting the lead story, an item in the middle and the last item. Also observe what the broadcaster is wearing. The next day, try and recall the three news items and the newscaster's clothes. Don't be surprised if you find you easily remember the colour of the tie worn by the newsreader, but not the lead story. Television has a worrying ability to focus an audience's attention wrongly. It's my job to show you how to redirect it.

Just as changing technology in newspapers has revolutionized that industry, so too has television been affected. With the introduction of ENG (electronic news gathering), a form of instant video recording, to television, the time taken to record, edit and broadcast a news item has been drastically reduced. The equipment is much lighter, the film doesn't have to be processed in a laboratory and the crews are staffed by fewer people. Its introduction has meant that a single crew can now cover up to three news stories in a day; again, in theory, tripling your chances of getting yourself in front of those passive millions.

Radio

The late 1980s have seen the renaissance of radio, with several independent stations going public and others taking advantage of the split frequency – which essentially means being able to run two radio stations for the price of one, and in theory attracting two different audiences and two different advertising revenues. Yet again, more opportunities for you to get your message across.

To date there are 99 independent local stations and 38 local BBC ones. National radio is covered by Radios 1, 2, 3, 4 and 5. In the next few years, Home Office permitting, we are likely to see a rapid growth in specialist radio stations, the first of which was the London incremental commercial station, Jazz

FM, followed by Melody Radio (easy listening for the over-fifties) and Kiss FM (dance music and soul). By the early 1990s there will probably also exist three national independent radio stations.

Radio, unlike television, doesn't have to vie so hard for your attention. It forms an immediate and intimate bond with the listener, whilst leaving the rest of the body free to engage in other activities. Radio enthusiasts always argue that the very lack of pictures is its great strength, the visual absence giving free rein to the imagination.

However, just as visual distraction on television can be a pitfall, *lack* of it on radio can also be an obstacle. If the speaker is hesitant or unclear, or speaks clumsily, no amount of listener intimacy will sustain the relationship.

Newsprint

The most remarkable change in the fortunes of the media has been the proliferation of newspapers. Apart from providing the industry with months of incestuous news, the breakthrough in printing technology, pioneered by Eddy Shah (founder and former owner of *Today*) and quickly followed by Rupert Murdoch (proprietor of *The Times* and *The Sun*), broke the stranglehold of the print unions and enabled newspapers to be produced more cheaply than ever before. Fleet Street became a geographical wasteland, and the 'hacks' have had to find new watering holes in such far-flung regions as the Isle of Dogs and Vauxhall.

However, as far as the public is concerned, the choice is wider than ever. Nearly fifteen million people buy a newspaper every day, and over seventeen million at the weekend. In the last four years alone, eight new newspapers have been launched, the two most successful being the *Independent* (circulation 496,890) and *Today* (circulation 612,060).* *Sunday*

---

* These and subsequent circulation figures are for August 1989, from the Audit Bureau of Circulation.

Today, News on Sunday and *The Post* didn't fare as well, but this didn't deter the backers of the *Sunday Correspondent* or the *Independent on Sunday*.

Newspapers are just as much slaves to fashion as their readers, which may account for the outbreak of colour supplement fever in the late 1980s. Although readers didn't complain overmuch, it seems that the industry had overlooked the rebellion of its foot soldiers – the boys and girls whose job it is to deliver the mountains of newsprint. The *Sunday Times* acted with alacrity by launching a design competition to overcome the problem.*

The battle for readers is fierce, particularly as daily sales have fallen by 400,000 and Sunday sales by 900,000 in the past decade, which probably accounts for even a quality paper like *The Times* introducing 'Portfolio', an upmarket bingo. Although they will tell you otherwise, a general reading of the statistics available tends to show a fairly consistent number of readers who, from time to time, switch allegiance.

The newspaper industry in Britain is divided into two categories: the daily qualities (*The Times, Guardian, Independent, Financial Times* and *Telegraph*) and the daily tabloids (*Sun, Daily Mirror, Today, Daily Mail, Daily Express, Morning Star* and so on). The circulation figures make interesting reading, if only to demonstrate that the majority of people who buy newspapers want it served up 'shocking' and 'simple':

Sun	4,073,102
Daily Mirror	3,137,778
Daily Mail	1,731,960
Daily Express	1,567,055
Daily Telegraph	1,104,004

* The winning trolley design by Tosh Winters is about to be manufactured and will be sold at cost price to newsagents.

Daily Star	886,460
Daily Record	772,331
Today	612,060
Independent	496,890
Guardian	418,158
The Times	416,187
Financial Times	196,142

The preference for prurience applies equally to Sunday reading tastes. The *News of the World* still outsells the *Sunday Times* by nearly four million an issue.

In Chapter 3 we take a much closer look at the style, approach and politics of all areas of the media, in preparation for an encounter. But it should be remembered that, politicians' squeals not withstanding, newspapers tend to be less coy about their political affiliations than are television or radio. The demographics of newspaper readers are also easier to define, which as far as you, the communicator, is concerned makes tailoring your message to a particular audience that much easier. A word of warning. Whilst the 'qualities' claim to be 'opinion formers', never forget that reputations can just as easily be made or lost in the *Daily Mirror*. Also, you are much more vulnerable to misinterpretation by a newspaper journalist than by a television or radio one.

How to deal confidently with the media

There might well be millions of years separating us from our tree-climbing ancestors, but our *subconscious* displays of anxiety or confidence are still much in evidence. For instance, just as an animal will always seek a prey weaker than itself, an interviewer will instinctively be much harder on the stumbling, inarticulate interviewee than on the one who exudes confidence. It is perhaps this unconscious reaction that has given rise to what is described as the 'gladiatorial' approach to interviews. Whatever the possible anthropological reasons, you'll find that most journalists opt for a confrontational style of interviewing rather than a seemingly open-ended one. From my own broadcasting experience, I know that unless I treat the interview as a contest, I will find it hard to arouse sufficient adrenalin to conduct a half-way stimulating interview.

It is, of course, one thing to recognize the need for confidence and quite another to display it, especially when you're in an unfamiliar and potentially hostile environment. There are two reasons why anyone approaching the media can afford to be innately confident:

- Hard as it may be to believe, they need you as much as you need them. The notion that reports are always about *other* people is an erroneous one. The media has a voracious appetite and the chances are that one of these days it may well come looking for *you*.
- You will invariably know 75 per cent more about your subject than any journalist. Agreed, reporters might give the impression of knowing as much as you, but believe me, they will be bluffing. They might, too, fix you with their X-ray eyes and trap you into thinking that they can read your mind – they can't. They're alert, poised, ready for the confrontation, but you're the one with the ammunition of knowledge.

Innate confidence, a rigorous approach to preparation, and

the assertion of your rights as an interviewee should equip you more than adequately for *any* media encounter. Before we look in detail at what we mean by 'preparation' and interviewees' 'rights', it's useful to turn the tables and find out what the interviewer wants from you.

What a reporter wants from an interviewee

Having previously brought you to a heightened pitch of mistrust, it's probably going to be a little difficult to persuade you that your interlocutor is as anxious as you that you should perform well. Remember what we said about reporters needing you as much as you need them, and how they react more positively to a confident interviewee than to a diffident one. It's also true that, if they're allowed to bask in the reflected glory of your competence, they will give you a much easier ride.

Joan Thirkettle, an experienced ITN reporter, knows exactly what she wants from an interviewee:

> I want them to answer the question. I don't want them to ramble or go off at a tangent, which a lot of people do either accidentally or deliberately. I want them to be well informed and talk to me as if we are having a conversation. Some people address me in blocked statements which immediately loses the interest of the viewer. What we really want is someone who can tell a story, and by so doing, draw the audience to them. David Bellamy is the finest exponent of what I mean. You don't have to know the first thing about botany to share his enthusiasm for his subject.

She adds a word of caution to the over-confident:

> I don't have any respect for people who are egocentric and go out of their way to score points over the reporter. The object of an interview is to inform and clarify. It should not be thought of as a battleground. Sometimes it turns into one when the

9

interviewee tries to intimidate a reporter whom he thinks is not as knowledgeable as he or she should be. Usually they are wrong, but even so the primary function of the interview is to communicate, not alienate.

Political television and radio broadcaster Ed Boyle stresses the thespian element of communicating:

> We want people who can speak with conviction, humour, passion and humanity – whatever the subject happens to be. We want the interviewee to use the occasion of the interview as an opportunity for a little bit of theatre. There is nothing worse than the *bland*, either for the reporter or the audience. No facet of human life, either in commerce or industry, needs to be dull. In fact, the alarm bells ring and we shout 'three cheers' when someone is able to bring some excitement to his message.

On Sunday, 1 October 1989, Dr Roger Williams, from King's College Hospital, Dulwich, was interviewed about the condition of a patient recovering from a liver transplant operation. Having assured the reporter that the patient's condition was satisfactory, he announced to the world, with no provocation, that the liver 'was producing bile beautifully'. No picture was needed; his word portrait, and the fact that he was being himself, drew the TV audience immediately to him.

Good and bad communicators

That speeches are spontaneous outpourings of silver-tongued wit and wisdom is a myth that politicians and comedians like to perpetuate. A remarkable exception to the spontaneity rule is US Vice-President Dan Quayle. Only the cruellest would suggest his brick-dropping is intentional. Addressing the United Negro College Fund, whose motto is 'A mind is a terrible thing to waste', he appeared to lose himself in a self-indicting verbal fog:

What a waste it is to lose one's mind or not to have a mind. How true that is.

Charged with fronting America's National Space Council, he found himself embarrassingly confused over names when filling in the details of the US mission to Mars. Buzz Aldrin, the second man on the moon, could not have relished being referred to as Buzz Lukens, a Congressman convicted of having sex with an under-age girl.

Very few people are skilled at improvization. Peter Ustinov and the late David Niven might have seemed to be telling a tale to an audience for the first time, but in reality each anecdote would have been rehearsed to perfection. The famous 'Ich bin ein Berliner' might have sounded like a spontaneous emotional statement from J.F. Kennedy, but it probably wasn't.

Just as with an interview, the way to make an impact with an audience is through preparation. Of course, a natural flair for gesture and an understanding of the cadence and rhythm of speech is important, but as the following extracts from accomplished speakers show, it's *what* is said that is so vital:

> In the past we have had a light which flickered, in the present we have a light which flames, and in the future there will be a light which shines over all the land and sea.
> (Winston Churchill speaking on the war with Japan, House of Commons, 8 December 1941.)

Across the Atlantic in Washington on the 28 August 1963, Martin Luther King gave hope to America's Negroes in what has become referred to as his 'I have a dream' speech:

> I have a dream that my four little children will one day live in a nation where they will not be judged by the colour of their skin but by the content of their character.
> I have a dream today.
> I have a dream that one day the state of Alabama, whose governor's lips are presently dripping with the words of inter-position and nullification, will be transformed into a situation where little black boys and black girls will be able to join hands with little white boys and little white girls and walk together as sisters and brothers.

I have a dream today.

Whatever pleasure the media derived from poking fun at former President Reagan's verbal slips, his ability to communicate via the televised presidential address was consummate. In his epitaph to the Challenger shuttle disaster in 1986, he moved a nation to tears when he said:

> We will never forget them, nor the last time we saw them this morning as they prepared for their journey and waved goodbye and slipped the surly bonds of Earth to touch the face of God.

Margaret Thatcher puts a great deal of store by her speech at the Conservative Party annual conference. In Brighton in 1988 she seemed to be on particularly fine form. On the environment:

> No generation has a freehold on this earth. All we have is a life tenancy with a full repairing lease. This government intends to meet the terms of that lease.

On Europe:

> We haven't worked all these years to free Britain from the paralysis of socialism only to see it creep in through the back door of bureaucracy from Brussels.

Not all of us may agree with Mrs Thatcher's principles, but her speeches are masterpieces of confidence, clarity and control.

A younger and more controversial communicator, but equally effective, is Anita Roddick, founder and Managing Director of The Body Shop. Her salty phrases and abundant enthusiasm have made her the darling of the media. And why not? She is energetic and passionate, and seems to embody the ethical side of capitalism.

> I'd rather wear out than rust to death. I have a great sense of mortality. This is not a dress rehearsal, so let's get on with it ... we have a great force for social change – who would have thought of a shop on the High Street educating consumers?

Anita Roddick could correct colour-blindness, such is the power of her imagery. When it comes to beauty, she succeeds because she talks about her products as things which

> cleanse, polish and protect the skin. I mean, how can you take a moisturizer seriously – it's not the body and blood of Christ, it's only oil and water.

Like all successful communicators, she invests every anecdote, however many times it may have been told before, with a sense of freshness. She's also refreshingly frank about her apparent ability to achieve:

> basically, it's the ability to cut the crap and get straight to the point.

The photo opportunity

 Although much has been said so far about the import-ance of the *word*, newspapers and television have also created a niche for the inarticulate.

Richard Branson, founder of Virgin records and multi-millionaire, is, by general consensus, a 'really nice chap'. But, and it's a big but, he is known to be shy, doesn't enjoy public speaking, and will avoid eye contact whenever he can. How is it, therefore, that he garners more column inches than cabinet ministers?

Branson has a magical flair for publicity. He seems to find *doing* something infinitely preferable to *talking* about it. Who will ever forget his stunt to cross the Atlantic by hot-air balloon? Even before the balloon had left American soil, Virgin pronounced the project a success in marketing terms. Branson himself estimated that, by the end of the flight, the Virgin name had been given the equivalent of £25 million of free advertising.

Questioned closely, people won't remember what Branson said, but they will recall his huge grin, tousled hair, sloppy jumpers and buccaneering spirit. By presenting so powerful a visual image, his verbal inadequacies can be forgiven.

You may not be so fortunate.

Remember

- The media needs you as much as you need it.
- You know more about your subject than they ever will.
- The more confident and fluent you appear, the cooler the hot seat will be.
- Thousands of pounds of free publicity beckon.

PART ONE
COURTSHIP

1 How to interest the media

As I will constantly stress in this book, unless you take a proactive attitude towards the media, you will end up either seething about all the free publicity going to your competitors, or regretting a poor personal performance caused by your own lack of forethought and preparation.

'HOME SECRETARY TO ACT ON PORN VIDEOS' was a headline which caused almost as much amusement as the now legendary 'FREDDIE STARR ATE MY HAMSTER'. Both were entirely misleading, but they achieved the sub-editor's aim of making the reader sit up and take notice. When trying to get the media interested in *you*, simply reverse the roles. If you can come up with a punchy headline that holds your attention for more than ten seconds, you've probably got a story. In other words, be prepared to shed all your intellectual pretensions and imagine you are communicating with an intelligent twelve-year-old.

Graham Lancaster is the co-founder and Chairman of a large London public relations company, Biss Lancaster. He comes into daily contact with the media, especially the press, and he is a devout believer in the philosophy of role reversal:

I approach the media by looking at what *they* want and not just at what we want to give them. Clients are in the business of selling their product or service to customers, and they must think of the media in the same sales relationship. So a journalist on a national newspaper needs to be categorized. Just as a manufacturer will understand the difference between a Sainsbury's buyer and a corner shop buyer, so you must understand the different approaches taken by, say, the Gardening Editors of *The Times* and the *Star*. The *Star* devotes far less space to gardening, because *Star* readers tend to have smaller gardens

17

than *Times* readers. Equally, as a businessman, you must understand that difference and target your communications the way you would target your sales literature.

So remember, when trying to interest the media:

- A story must always have an 'angle' or a 'peg': that is, a reason to run it. A 'peg' could be news of a bid or deal, the appointment of a new Chairman, the breaking of a record, or the publication of a book.
- The 'headline' should tell the story and the details should always have colour and memorable facts. Better to leave the reader or viewer with an *impression* than with a jumble of disconnected thoughts.
- No story should make more than *three* points.
- It must always be *positive*, but also frank. Journalists are wary of hype.
- Never forget that a story which originates at local level could quickly arouse national interest. Always devote as much care to a local story as you would to a national one.

Whom to approach

Most organizations leave the task of getting press coverage to the professionals. Public relations companies, in-house press offices and lobbyists can be more objective and have very thick skins. When you're not used to the vagaries of the media, it can be very hurtful to watch your story sink into oblivion or be distorted beyond recognition.

However, if you think that 'fortune favours the brave', you might well avoid the cost of consultants and go it alone. There are two invaluable directories which will give you the names, addresses and phone numbers of key media contacts.

Newspapers and magazines are comprehensively listed in the *Writers' and Artists' Yearbook* (published annually by A. & C. Black, currently priced £6.95). As well as the title, address and phone number of the publication, each entry will provide the name of the current editor and a brief description of the house style. Supposing your company had produced a new grip for a golf club, and you wanted to publicize the fact. A quick reference to the *Writers' and Artists' Yearbook* would tell you about the specialist golfing magazines, as well as advising you on the type and length of articles published.

Although the *Yearbook* has a section on radio and television, it contains nowhere near the detailed information found in the *Blue Book of British Broadcasting* (published by Tellex Monitors), a manual that lists every radio and television company in Britain (national and local), including names of key personnel and programming schedules. At £42 a copy it's not cheap, but in terms of the sheer value of detailed information it's a worthwhile investment. Just as in industry the key to getting something done is to find the person who can make a decision, so it is with the media. Really careful targeting is the only sure route to getting yourself or your product on the airwaves.

Many large organizations, especially public relations companies, subscribe to detailed media directories which are regularly updated. PIMS, PNA and Advance are the best known.

PIMS (4 St John's Place, London EC1M 4AH, telephone: 071–250 0870)

As well as offering a press-cutting service, PIMS publish a monthly directory of editorial contacts, divided into six sections:

- National newspapers: includes current affairs contacts on nationals, regional dailies and news agencies, e.g. News Editor.
- Trade and technical press (very useful contacts for press conferences). Twenty-three subject areas from finance to architecture. Within each section there are contacts for nationals, regionals, trade magazines and freelancers.
- Consumer section. Again, named contacts, covering women's magazines, gardening, sport, holidays, etc.
- TV and radio. Twenty-five sections including all BBC radio and TV and ILR (Independent Local Radio) and ITV stations,

19

and a range of contacts for both trade and technical and consumer subjects.
- Weekly newspaper section, broken down county by county.
- Facsimile numbers. This is a relatively new section, giving the Fax numbers for the previously mentioned outlets.

Entries for magazines include the circulation figures and frequency of publication.

PIMS UK Media Directory costs £75 for a one-off copy. A quarterly subscription (i.e. four copies a year) costs £149 a year, and a monthly subscription (all twelve copies) costs £215.

Advance (Theme Tree Ltd, 2 Prebendar Court, Oxford Road, Aylesbury, Bucks HP19 3EY, telephone: 0296 28585)

The *Advance Feature Directory* is aimed mainly at advertisers as it lists forthcoming features in magazines up to two months in advance, and editorial copy dates. It's published six times a year, and has 42 different subject sections. The subscription cost is £112 a year.

PNA (PNA Services Ltd, 13 Curtain Road, London EC2, telephone: 071–377 2521)

The *PNA Media Guide* covers all UK editorial media, which it divides into colour-coded sections, including city contacts. Each section provides a key contact to each publication. Names of more specialized journalists are given at the back of the directory. It's updated every six months and an annual subscription costs £165 for six copies. Its service is also available on a PC, which makes updating very simple.

The hierarchy in radio and television closely resembles that in the print medium. A radio station, for instance, will have a proprietor, chairman, chief executive or managing director, programme controller, producers, presenters, reporters, and engineers. However, unlike in television, there are no researcher jobs in radio. This always comes as a rude shock to an employee making the transition from television to radio.

Your official point of contact for either a radio or television programme is the producer. It is he or she who always determines programme content. If you already have a contact, by all means use it. If not, you should adopt the following procedure. Before making an approach, make sure you have his or her correct name and that you're familiar with the programme. I am sometimes confused with the petite blonde comedienne Sandra Dickinson, and it amuses me to see the flicker of disappointment on the faces of some of my male guests when entering the radio studio.

Radio and television producers are extremely busy and don't appreciate unexpected calls. They will, however, take note of a well-written press release (see p. 24). Depending on the frequency of the programme, always deliver the press release to the producer at least one week before the event is due to take place. Give him or her a day to assimilate the information and then make your phone call.

Try to be accommodating. Remember it's free publicity, and you don't want to jeopardize that opportunity by quibbling over who pays for the taxi. All journalists operate the 'instant assimilation' approach to research. They scan two or three press cuttings and confidently assume they are qualified to conduct the interview. Pamper this ego and provide them with some carefully selected background material – a brief biography, a favourable review of the product (even journalists are impressed by seeing something in print), a pithy quote or anecdote and, but *sparingly please*, some statistics. Don't antagonize the producer by including a list of suggested questions.

If your story has a news rather than a feature angle, you should approach the news editor rather than a specific producer. For instance, London's all-talk commercial radio station LBC Newstalk 97.3 FM, takes its news stories from IRN – Independent Radio News. If the story is sufficiently interesting, a reporter will be asked to provide not only a 20–30 second 'byte' for the news, but a longer 2–3 minute piece for a programme.

Although news editors do, of course, respond to press

releases, they tend to get most of their news leads via the various wire services.

The Press Association (85 Fleet Street, London EC4P 4BE, telephone: 071–353 7440)

The Press Association is one of the few remaining Fleet Street habitués, and is essentially a home news agency, providing news, sport and photographs to both the metropolitan and the provincial press, and it is the agency you're most likely to use. It acts as a kind of clearing house for news, taking in stories from many different sources, writing them up in a crisp, succinct style and distributing them to its subscribers.

Whereas Press Association information used to be available only by teleprinter, nowadays it's also produced in computer view-data form. The Press Association will always receive the details of your story, but they are not obliged to publish the information. If you contact them by phone, you should ask for 'copytakers', and if you're writing, you should address your communication to the News Editor. Determined publicists will monitor PA output and push their editors to include the item if it appears to have been overlooked. Be careful that you don't wear out the welcome mat by being too persistent. Remember, you might want to go back tomorrow with a bigger story. The Press Association is open 24 hours a day, 365 days a year. If you are aiming your story at the nationals, you need to have contacted the Association by 3 p.m. at the latest, the day before.

Reuters (85 Fleet Street, London EC4P 4AJ, telephone: 071–250 1122)

Reuters is part of Associated Press (not to be confused with the Press Association), and disseminates international news, operating from the same address as the Press Association.

Universal News Service (UNS), (Communications House, Gough Square, London EC4P 4DP, telephone 071–353 5200)

UNS is a commercial organization syndicating news stories paid for by the client. Although it offers much greater editorial control, like the other services it carries no guarantee of usage. UNS is best known for distributing press releases through its computerized newswire network to the national press, major regional morning and evening newspapers and the broadcasting services. In addition, it can distribute news internationally. Costings vary according to where you wish your story to be sent. Their National Newswire service distributes news to 153 newsrooms in England, Scotland and Wales, and current costs are £185 for up to 300 words and £40 for each additional 100 words. The earlier you send your news to UNS, the better is the chance of publication. For example, stories for Monday papers can be sent on Friday or Saturday, and will be networked on Sunday, when editors are searching for material. This news would be repeated early on Monday, for the evening papers.

To woo or not to woo

 The image of the journalist in old raincoat, with collar turned up and spiral notebook in hand, now belongs to the film archives. These days they tend to look more like bankers.

As with any organization, the more people you know, the more chance you have of jumping the queue. And although journalists may appear cynical, they can seldom resist the conspiratorial approach that promises a story. Unfortunately, because their industry is now geographically scattered, the traditional meeting places of Fleet Street, like El Vino's and the City Golf Club, are seldom used, and it's quite difficult to persuade journalists to travel to the West End just for the pleasure of your company. You won't find this nearly such an obstacle with the provincial press or television people, who always seem to have the time.

It is very unwise to attempt to bribe a media person, or, as the taxman would say, to offer something that could be seen as a taxable benefit. However, there is a discernible trend towards presenting a press release in an unusual way to ensure that the journalist's attention is engaged. I'd draw the line at having your missive delivered by a girl on roller skates, because that could give the impression of frivolity, but something presented with a touch of wit and style would certainly impress the journalist and increase your chances of media coverage.

How to write a press release

 Journalists or editors, be it radio, press or television, want two things from you. One is a prerequisite, and the other almost as essential.

Firstly, they need access to the same story as their competitors, which they would probably have gained either from the Press Association wire service or from your press release. Then, once they've got the basic facts, they will want a completely *different* story from everyone else. This is known in the media as the *angle*. Whilst it is obviously a journalist's job to create his or her own angle to a story, it certainly does no harm to create one of your own.

Not everyone subscribes to Winston Churchill's opinion that people only want to read one A4 sheet, triple-spaced. But as a general rule a press release shouldn't be longer than two A4 sheets.

Eighty per cent of press releases are thrown away, so you must capture your audience with an arresting headline.

'FUNFULL TOYS OPENS NEW FACTORY'

doesn't make as great an impact as

'FUNFULL TOYS CREATES 30 NEW JOBS'.

Similarly, a journalist's eye would be much more drawn to

'WILLIAM SHAKESPEARE – WINNER OF BIGGEST
BOOK CASH PRIZE'

than to

'WILLIAM SHAKESPEARE WINS BOOK PRIZE'.

In other words, you must always write your press release from the journalist's viewpoint, presenting the facts with succinct fluency. Always make sure that you provide a contact name and telephone number and, having done so, make sure that the person who answers that number is briefed and ready to take a journalist's call. Unless a reporter is chasing *you*, he or she won't call again if you can't give the answers first time around.

Remember

- Be *proactive* not *reactive* with the media.
- Always find a *named* contact. 'To whom it may concern' missives will go straight in the bin.
- Think in headlines, especially when writing a press release.
- There's no such thing as 'off the record'.
- Find the best spokesperson.
- Make sure you obtain a copy of your performance.

25

2 The press conference

It is the tragedy of the world that no-one knows what he doesn't know; and the less a man knows, the more sure he is that he knows everything.
Joyce Carey, *Art and Reality*, 1958

Preparing for a press conference

Holding a press conference can be a very effective way of both saving time and money, and killing *several* birds with one stone. You might consider holding one for the following reasons:

- To launch a product, a book, a fund, a prize, a charity or a political campaign.
- To disclose company news – a merger, a management buyout, a resignation, a recruitment drive, the workers' fightback.
- To clear the air, explain a controversy, lay a rumour.
- To reveal the scoop of the century – a newly-discovered play by Shakespeare, the real site of Camelot, Lord Lucan's whereabouts.

There is no point in holding one unless:

- You have something to announce that can't be adequately described in a press release.
- You have something to say that will benefit from detailed elaboration.
- You are adequately prepared to answer supplementary questions confidently.
- You choose the timing and venue with care.

26

When to hold a press conference

Avoid days of public importance, like Budget day, polling days or public holidays.

If you want to try and hit the evening papers, your deadline is about noon. Early evening television news shows need at least two hours to get the material edited and ready for transmission. If you do have the confidence to cut it that fine, it will certainly ensure that your story is topical and could come fairly high in the running order (the sequence in which stories appear).

There is a tendency for reporters and camera crews to begin shooting at the start of a press conference, which means that the strength of your introduction is vital (see p. 36). Film crews are always in a hurry, so the easier you can make their job in terms of editing, the more likely you are to be reported faithfully and flatteringly.

Incentives

On 25 January 1961, J.F. Kennedy became the first US President to allow his press conferences to be televised. Attendance figures rocketed, not least because it gave the journalists the opportunity to become stars in their own right. How long, one wonders, had been spent on honing the question to give the impression of effortless fluency?

In the 1960s and 1970s, it was customary to ply reporters and photographers with food and drink, and to fly them off to exotic locations. These inducements tend to be frowned upon today except, it seems, for magazine journalists who, because they only go to press once a week or once a month, have far more time to avail themselves of an all-expenses-paid trip to Tangier or Bologna. However, it's as well to remember that the media have to eat, so the offer of good food and drink in the invitation to your press conference seldom goes amiss.

How to select a spokesperson

My long experience in the field of industrial videos has made me very adept at persuading the chairman of a company that, despite his position, he is not necessarily the right person to

represent his company on film. Some people are born communicators. Others are not. If you are going to have a successful relationship with the media, egos must be sacrificed to
common sense. Find the best communicator in your company
and groom him or her for stardom.

There now exist a growing number of companies which,
like my own, specialize in media training. During a typical one-
day seminar, the client is taken through all the rigours of
radio, press and television interviews, and is shown how each
discipline puts an item together and what it will try and do to
its victims. The client will almost certainly have to do simulated
television and radio interviews, and perhaps a telephone one,
all of which are recorded for subsequent analysis. Unlike the
real interview, every trainee's exercise will be closely assessed,
with attention paid to both physical and mental performance.

Despite the element of role-play, most trainees find their first
television interview extremely stressful. It is *always* a shock to
see oneself on television – it seems to add about ten years and
ten pounds to all of us, and it is not kind to body language.
But training is a salutary experience. Everyone improves and,
because of its confidentiality, it's as cathartic as a confessional.

What to expect

You will experience precisely the same sense of panic half an
hour before the start of your press conference as you do before
a party at home. Will anyone turn up? Will too many people
arrive? Have we enough brochures/chairs/ashtrays/glasses?

What you can be sure of is that many of those who promised
to attend won't and, conversely, some who didn't bother to
reply will. The one journalist on whom you had been pinning
so much will fail to materialize. Many will be late and some
will leave early, and you'll probably find yourself left with the
dregs, drones and bores to whom you must be civil and engag-
ing to the bitter end.

Still think it's worth it?

The key to a successful press conference is meticulous *preparation*, and we'll now look at some aspects of this in more detail.

The venue

Use a little intelligence when choosing the venue for your press conference. Try and make it as accessible as possible for everyone. Ever since newspapers moved away from Fleet Street, journalists in London have been prepared to make the effort to attend conferences so long as they are in a reasonably central location. Regional journalists are far more used to the inconvenience of distance.

Unless your press conference includes a tour of your new plant or offices, it's usually best to opt for the anonymity and efficiency of a central hotel. Many hotels rely on the conference trade for their profits, particularly out of season, and most of them should be more than willing to meet your requirements at a competitive price.

Whichever venue you select, make sure that the room you choose is the right size, has a small platform at one end, can accommodate the use of visual aids (slides, overhead projectors, videos or flip charts) and has microphone facilities if you need them.

It's attention to detail that can make or break a press conference. What's the use of a lectern that obscures half your face? And it's equally distracting to have a light shining directly in your eyes. If you haven't checked out the facilities beforehand, you can hardly blame the hotel when things go wrong.

You must take great care over the seating arrangements. As a general rule, the conference speakers should be seated at a table, on a slightly raised dais. A lectern with appropriate aids should be set up near to the table, so they can be easily used for the formal opening and closing presentations.

Visual aids

A visual aid is principally there for your audience and *not* for you. It is both tempting and distracting to use a visual aid as a prompt. All too often you'll see the summary of someone's speech displayed behind them on a screen and the speaker spending more time addressing the image than the audience.

29

Just as your speech should contain symbol and metaphor, so should your visual aids.

It's a good idea to have your company logo displayed as your first image when the invitees take their seats. What follows is up to you, but your approach should be simple and clear. Don't be afraid to use symbols, cartoons, coloured blocks or single words. They all make an immediate impact on your audience. Complicated criss-crossing graphs that look like Route 66 at night are of no use at all. Nor are detailed quotes from the Company Report or the much-favoured bar charts that leave you marvelling at the wonders of computer graphics, but none the wiser as to what they mean.

Whichever visual aids you decide to use, it is imperative that you make sure beforehand that they have been rehearsed. It won't amuse anybody when a slide appears upside down or you try and separate a piece of acetate (perspex) from its interleaving tissue paper. It's possible to buy acetates with generous cardboard surrounds, which are much easier to handle. Make sure you know how the projector works, which button focuses and which activates the next slide, and that the microphone is at the right height and won't emit an ear-splitting screech when switched on. Prevent the small mishaps and you will ensure no loss of points as far as your competence and credibility are concerned.

Speakers are often very uncertain how to refer to a visual aid. I'm a great believer that the fewer props you have to carry, the better. As long as your body doesn't obscure the image, it's usually perfectly effective to point with the index finger rather than use a baton or 'light stick'.

OVERHEADS

An overhead image is created by placing a piece of acetate on to a light box in front of you. Its advantage is that, using special pens, the speaker can draw on the acetate while talking. An element of suspense can also be created by only revealing part of the sheet at a time. The obvious disadvantages are the initial difficulties most people have in handling them easily and the fact that few speakers can think and speak at the same time, let alone draw. The light from the box also tends to obliterate the speaker's facial features completely.

35 mm PROJECTORS

If you're going to use slides, it's as well to have them professionally made. You know how easily bored you are by other people's holiday/wedding/anniversary snaps, and you can be quite certain that your audience will react in just the same way to an ill-prepared slide show. Better to have too few than too many. Try to use the slides as if you're building up a story. This will often mean the use of the same slide more than once, but don't try to economize by thinking you can effortlessly flick back to the place of origin. You will most likely lose your place and run the risk of heckling from the floor (see p. 45). If you're feeling really confident, break the monotony of your presentation by deliberately including a completely *inappropriate* slide – you at the staff dance slightly the worse for wear, or, even better, with a stunningly beautiful woman. Feign embarrassment at its unexpected inclusion and move on swiftly. You'll bring the house down. This ruse should only be attempted by the supremely confident.

FLIP CHARTS

As anyone who has ever used one will know, flip charts assume unfamiliar characteristics in moments of stress. During rehearsal, you've efficiently and fairly quietly managed to turn over the jumbo sheets individually. Come the actual presentation, a gremlin seems to have glued the sheets together. The felt-tip pens fall to the floor, or suddenly dry up, and a wag from the back of the hall (the one who has already asked you to speak up) claims he can't see.

VIDEO

Despite the fact that many people will, at some time or other, have seen themselves on video, a moving image is still by far the most effective visual aid – so long as it's a professional production. Ten minutes of the head and shoulders of your chairman won't do. A well-paced video or use of split screens will.

If you do opt for video demonstrations, make sure that you have enough monitors in the room and that the volume is sufficient. If people have to crane to catch the image, you can be certain they won't catch the story.

AUTO-CUE

Most people realize that presenters and newsreaders on television are not blessed with photographic memories, but are reading from auto-cue – a small TV monitor placed just below the camera on which the presenter's script silently appears. Operated by a technician, the flow of the printed words follows the speed of the presenter's delivery.

A similar system has been evolved for platform speakers. Known unofficially as a 'sincerity screen', a small glass panel is placed on a slim stand in front of the speaker. Reflected on to the screen, just as in a television studio, is the text, again controlled by an operator who will follow the speaker's speed. Leading politicians often opt for two glass screens – one either side of them – so they can enhance the appearance of spontaneity by appearing to talk to all their audience, not just the ones straight ahead of them.

Whether you use one or two screens, the secret is not to rely on them too heavily. If you do, the effect will be worse than if you read from notes. The trick to their successful use lies in your text. Don't write in every single word, but do write in a few pauses and even gestures and stage instructions. Auto-cue print can offer you upper or lower case and underlining, but it cannot highlight words. You must, from time to time, have the confidence to look away from the screen and at your audience. Eye contact with a group of people is just as important as it is with one person.

The most natural way to perform is to use your 'sincerity screen' with discretion, backed up by your three main points and a few supplementaries written clearly on index cards. If you must use A4 sheets of paper, get them mounted on to medium-stiff card – so much easier to handle, and silent. You might also try typing your speech like a film script.

A large portion of the left-hand side of the paper is left clear, as if you were to include camera instructions, and the right contains the script (see page 34). The less horizontal distance the eye has to cover, the quicker the absorption of the material. Always type your speech in not less than one and a half spacing with plenty of highlighting. If you do plan to use auto-cue at your press conference, it is well worth rehearsing the technique beforehand.

HAND-OUTS

Few of us have grown out of the childhood tradition of expecting a present when we leave a party. Pander to this absurdity by always making sure those who attend your press conference have something to take away with them. At the very least they should be given a file containing a copy of the main speeches and your company brochure and, if relevant, photographs.

If you can include samples of your product or examples of objective assessment, so much the better. Free pens, notepads and matches still seem to be appreciated. They also act as a useful reminder of your identity as journalists begin to pen their purple prose.

The Invitation

Because press conferences are sometimes called at short notice and journalists don't always answer an invitation, it's very difficult to estimate how many might attend. A very general rule of thumb seems to be that you can expect about a third of all those you invite to turn up. They may not be the ones you'd like to be there, but at least they occupy some of the seats.

You should take care over the wording and presentation of the invitation. A cursory note to the 'Features Editor' is less likely to provoke a response than a personalized one. It's a small detail, but have the guest's name hand-written rather

DAVID BROWN/SALES CONFERENCE

Smile   Hello, and good evening.

Pause

                         My name is David Brown and, as some
                         of you will know, I'm chairman of

Slide 1:
  (Company logo)   Ideas Unlimited,
                         a company that, in the last five
                         years, has developed no less than
                         three innovative ideas to make the
                         driver's life easier.

Pause

Slide 2:   Our Inflatable Car Seat.

Pause

Slide 3:   Adjustable Windscreen Wipers.
                         And the one that seemed to
                         cause the greatest stir...

Pick up object

Pause and smile   At first the public proved rather
                         uncertain about this oddity, but
                         once they realized its versatility
                         and its practicality, the product
                         became an immediate success.

Slide 4:   As this slide shows, our profit
                         margins have increased by 25 per
                         cent since we introduced it...

than printed on the invitation. Always give about ten days' notice.

On the whole, it's best to keep the invitation clear and to the point. The journalist wants to know *why* he or she has been invited (announcement of interim figures, publication of book, introduction of celebrity, promise of surprise), *when* it will take place, *where* and *at what time*. Always include a brief press release, taking care to build on the surprise element promised by the calling of the conference, a map of directions and, most important of all, a *contact number*. Often journalists won't be able to attend the conference themselves, but will note it in their diary and follow it up afterwards with a phone call.

Make sure you keep a copy of the invitation list, so that those who fail to reply can be discreetly chased nearer to the day. It's surprising how that little extra effort will often result in attendance.

The top table

It's not unusual to find that a company fields several speakers at a press conference. Doing so adds some often much-needed variety to the presentations. Make sure everyone is assembled on the platform *before* the conference starts. Seat the Chairman in the middle, with the lieutenants on either side. *Never* seat any of your spokespeople in the front row of the audience. Bringing them up on stage will interrupt the flow of the proceedings and embarrass the spokesperson. Make sure that there are plenty of notepads and pencils, and that there's lots of water.

When to begin

Even though you think ITN may turn up, you should start the first part of your conference not later than ten minutes after the stated time. Be sure, as people assemble, that they are given a press pack and are asked to sign the visitor's book. If there is to be an informal session afterwards, it's very useful for everybody to wear identity badges. Subtle colour coding is also a good idea. Green spot for the press, red for staff and blue for dignitaries.

Try to be as accommodating as your patience will allow to television and radio crews. They need to be at the front to get the pictures and the sound. As they usually have to be away before their colleagues, make sure that you take their questions earlier, rather than later.

Conducting a press conference

The verb 'conducting' is used deliberately. Someone from your company, preferably you, must take complete charge of the press conference, from the planning stage to the follow-up. Don't be lulled into a false sense of security and assume that you'll automatically repeat last week's successful performance at the sales conference. Your board and your sales team have a vested interest in listening with rapt attention. The media doesn't. Be wary, too, of in-house jargon. 'Apparel garments' might be perfectly acceptable language to the 'rag trade', but people in the media talk about clothes.

There are three main parts to the press conference:

- the formal presentations
- the question and answer session
- light refreshments and the informal press conference

The formal presentations

As I suggested earlier, you have to be in *complete control* of the proceedings, and you will only achieve that heady sense of power if you are – yes, you're catching on – *prepared*.

The presentation or introduction is *the* most important part of a press conference. If you fail to grab the audience's attention in your opening remarks, it is unlikely that you'll make much subsequent impact. Effective presentation is not difficult to achieve, so long as you stick to a tried and tested formula:

1 Greeting
2 Business
3 Outline of speech
4 Body of speech
5 Summary
6 Conclusion

(1) GREETING

First bring the meeting to order or you'll never get off to a positive start. If you need to bang a gavel, do so loudly.

> Ladies and gentlemen, I know you've all got deadlines to meet, so let's get started. My name is Peter Black and, as most of you know, I'm Chief Executive of Sound Investments Incorporated. I'd like to introduce you to my team. On my left ...

(2) BUSINESS

When it comes to being organized, adults are very child-like. They need to be reminded of certain basic facts before they can settle to more important matters. Even if you've told them before in the press release, tell them again at the conference:

● how long the conference will last;
● how much time has been allowed for questions;
● whether there's any back-up material available;
● whether there will be refreshments.

(3) OUTLINE OF SPEECH

Have I got to listen to the *history* of Sound Investments Inc. (in which case I'll leave now), or are you going to tell me something interesting about your mid-term figures and the future of the economy? Give me some indication and I might pay more attention.

(4) BODY OF SPEECH

Just as in an interview you should never try to make more than three main points, the same rule applies to giving a presentation. John May has taught thousands of business people to overcome their nerves and speak in public. 'You can use the simple arithmetic of the hand to measure length,' he says. 'One, two, three, enough, too much.'

Treat each main point as a separate entity, with a beginning, a middle and an end. Each summing-up is particularly important to combat the drooping eyelid and nodding head syndrome. You will skilfully compensate for any lapses of concentration by a succinct summary after each point. Don't forget that to err is human. If you do make a mistake during your speech, don't let it unhinge you. Smile, apologise and carry on.

(5) SUMMARY

Not only should you summarize each section; you should also, as you get towards the end of the speech, summarize generally, and this will lead you naturally towards your concluding remarks.

> Ladies and gentlemen, that's the end of the 'official party line' as it were; we'd be delighted to take questions from the floor for about fifteen minutes, after which time I do hope you'll join us for drinks and a light buffet lunch next door where we can continue our conversation. Thank you.

Allow about thirty seconds for your audience to prepare itself for the next phase and then re-establish control by taking the first question.

LENGTH OF SPEECH

The formal element of a press conference shouldn't run for longer than about 45 minutes. Allowing 10 minutes for settling down, and 15 to 30 minutes for questions, your introductory piece shouldn't be much longer than 10 minutes. Believe me, in most cases that is *quite* long enough.

TIMING A SPEECH

Good speeches are not plucked from the ether. They are carefully researched, planned and rehearsed. Those rousing extracts we read in Chapter 1 were all examples of finely tuned oratory.

A very simple way to get a rough estimate of the length of your speech is to type it up on an A4 sheet of paper, double spacing, with 1 inch margins either side. You'll type approximately 30 lines with about 12 words to a line. As the ideal speed of speech for presentations is about 160 words a minute, a page of text comes to about two and a half minutes. Therefore, four pages of text should take about 10 minutes to deliver.

Successful public speaking

William Gladstone, former Liberal Prime Minister, had six rules for successful public speaking:

● simple words
● short sentences
● distinct diction
● testing one's arguments beforehand
● knowledge of subject
● watching the audience

There are very few people who enjoy public speaking. It makes most of us feel extremely exposed and vulnerable, highlighting unconscious weaknesses which we reveal when addressing an audience: forgetting to look up from our notes, swaying nervously from side to side, fiddling with a pen or pencil, or jangling the coins in our pocket – all maddening bad habits in a speaker. We've all strained to hear the sotto speaker and to keep up with the one who gabbles throughout. We've longed to tell someone to take their hand away from their mouth or stop fiddling with their hair. Unless you are careful, the next time you have to make a speech, you'll find yourself making some, if not all, of those mistakes.

THE SPEAKER AS PERFORMER

Speaking in public is all about giving a performance and giving you the opportunity to be positive. Anything less, and you will fail to make an impact on your audience. Anyone who has the temerity to address a group of people must accept that that group is expecting to be *entertained*. Make them laugh, make them cry, make them cross, but *never bore them*.

A common recurring nightmare is the one where you're about to go on stage and you still don't know your lines. If you haven't rigorously prepared the text of your speech, that nightmare could well become reality. To continue the acting analogy, think of the way you're dressed as your costume, your speech as your part in the play, and the venue as the stage. If you can somehow convince yourself that you are only *acting*, your performance will automatically improve. Simply distancing yourself from you will bring a little much-needed objectivity to the proceedings.

Your props

● lectern
● visual aids
● notes
● water
● auto-cue (possibly)

Compared with what is needed for an average theatrical production, you've really got very little to worry about. But do make sure you're familiar with whatever props you do intend to use and that they work.

Your clothes

The same rules apply when choosing what to wear for a public presentation as they do for television (see p. 121). Be smart, clean and, above all, comfortable.

Your part

The first thirty seconds of your speech must be made without the use of notes, and from thereon in try and use them as little as possible. They should be there merely as a prompt, *not* as a script.

EYE CONTACT

This is just as important when talking to a group of people as it is when you're addressing one person. In order to give the impression that you're talking to everyone in a room, try the windscreen wiper technique. Take your gaze from the left, to the centre, to the right and back again. It will feel artificial at first, but it is certainly very effective, even if there are bright lights shining in your eyes. Don't forget – even though you can't see your audience, they can see you, so it is important to maintain a varied eye contact whatever the circumstances.

SIGNPOSTS

Although you will have told your audience in your intro-duction the main purpose of your speech and for how long you intend to talk, further signposts of progress will have to come from you. Unlike the written word, a live audience doesn't have the benefit of chapter headings, bold text or paragraphs.

For instance, how do you let an audience know when you're moving on to another aspect of your speech? As when dealing with a difficult question in interview, you employ the *bridging* technique:

In the last five minutes, I've taken you very briefly through the history of our company. Now we come to the moment you've all been waiting for – the revelation of our plans for the 1990s ...

41

THE THREE PS

How do you emphasize a point? How do you stop your audience falling asleep? There are numerous verbal tricks we will deal with in a moment, but first it is important to get to grips with the 'three Ps' of public speaking:

- pitch
- pace
- pause

Pitch

The more nervous we are, the higher the pitch of our voice. As a deep voice tends to carry more authority than a very light one, it's as well to record your own voice before you embark on any public speaking. If it sounds tinny, refer to the breathing exercises in Chapter 5 (p. 138). Control of the inhalation and exhalation of air automatically leads to control of the pitch of the voice.

Nothing is more tedious to the ear than a monotone, so decide beforehand which parts of your speech require you to speak up and which can be delivered very quietly.

Pace

By varying the pace at which you speak, you will be able to identify clearly to an audience those aspects of your speech which are more important than others. For instance, if you're recapping, you can speed up. If, on the other hand, you want your audience really to take notice, then have the confidence to slow right down.

Pause

A pause, at the right moment, can make a dramatic impact on an audience:

> We will continue the search until every can of infected soup has been found [pause] and I mean every can.

42

Using pauses wisely not only helps to emphasize a point, it also gives you and your audience a moment's breathing space.

GESTURE

When the botanist David Bellamy was first introduced to our television screens, I'm sure there were many who smiled at his flamboyant gestures. But he persisted in the use of them and they are now an essential part of his presentation. *Don't be afraid of overdoing the gestures – it is unlikely that you ever will.* In fact, gestures during a presentation need to be much more generous than when you're in a television or radio studio. Use your fingers to count your points. Clench your fist to indicate determination. Point at your audience to assert your authority. Open the palms of your hands to emphasize your honesty. Reach out your arms to embrace your audience. Remember, though, *don't* cross your arms in front of you, or have your hands in your pockets or clenched over your genitals.

VERBAL TRICKS

Verbal tricks are usually used not only to break the monotony of a speech, but for emphasis.

Concluding with an opposite

An effective way of making a strong point is to list a number of similar points and conclude with an opposite:

> We will bring down inflation. We will maintain employment levels. We will remain loyal to our European allies. We will *not* let the Opposition deter us from our task.

Repetition

Repetition of a word can also be effective. Anthony Eden, during a television broadcast to the nation explaining why he was sending troops to Suez, used the technique to considerable effect:

43

All my life I have been a man of *peace*, working for *peace*, striving for *peace*, negotiating for *peace* . . .

Abraham Lincoln during the Gettysburg Address in 1863 employed the same technique:

this nation under God shall have a new birth of freedom and . . . the government *of the people, by the people, for the people,* shall not perish from the earth.

The rhetorical question

This is a very effective way of breaking a speech into digestible chunks. The speaker wants to let his audience know that he's about to summarize before moving on to his second main point. He introduces a rhetorical question as a way of so doing:

So, ladies and gentlemen, what does the information I've revealed to you this afternoon really tell you about our industry? [Pause] I suggest to you that . . .

The pronoun

Audiences like to feel involved with a speaker and they like to be flattered:

Now, I know most of you in this room today will remember the challenge we faced this time last year . . .

If you actually *know* someone in the audience, even better:

Peter, good of you to come today. You'll remember our conversation about this time last year when we managed to . . .

Humour

Unless you are really confident about telling jokes *don't*. But *do* bring in humour whenever you can, especially during the opening moments of your speech, even if it's something as trivial as:

Ladies and gentlemen, thank you all for joining us this morning.

44

I'm sorry the bar won't be open until *after* I've finished speaking. I'm told that's for my benefit rather than yours ...

However bleak the news Winston Churchill often had to impart during the Second World War, he never missed an opportunity to introduce humour. Reporting to his War Cabinet, he once said:

> ... and when I warned them that Britain would fight on alone, whatever they did, their generals told their Prime Minister and his divided Cabinet that in three weeks England will have her neck wrung like a chicken. [Long pause] Some chicken. [Long pause] Some neck.

Dealing with interruptions

Almost as unnerving as losing your place is being interrupted. Even if the interruption is genuine – for instance, someone is asking you to speak up – your confidence and composure will evaporate. The golden rule is: *always* take heed of an interruption (it can be turned to your advantage), but *never* rise to the bait. If someone can't hear, immediately depart from your script and acknowledge the interruption:

> I'm sorry you can't hear me, particularly as it means you may have missed some of my pearls of wisdom. Is that better?

You've acknowledged the problem, corrected it *and* strengthened your bond with your audience.

If the interruptions become more boisterous, you must *never* let yourself get out of control. Deal with hecklers swiftly, confidently and with humour:

> The gentleman in the yellow sweater appears to be angling for my job, but he knows as well as I do the time for him to make his point comes later, not now. So I will do a deal with you, sir. If you won't interrupt me, I won't interrupt you when it comes to your turn.

If these polite, but firm, tactics don't work, you have every right to ask a heckler to leave. *Never forget, you're the one in control.*

The question and answer session

This is where the fun begins. It's back to those principles of *confidence, clarity* and *control*.

During preparation for your press conference, you will, of course, have spent some time *anticipating* the questions you're likely to be asked. Decide at that point who is going to deal with certain issues if they are raised. There is nothing more frustrating for an audience than watching a panel trying to decide who will take a question. Make sure that one person acts as a filter for *all* that questions and that he or she always takes a note of the questioner's name and organization. Not only is it important to know with whom you are about to speak, but it's useful to have a name to follow up.

If the hall requires a roving microphone, make sure that someone competent operates it. Again, do remember that TV and radio usually have earlier deadlines than the press, so try and take their questions first. If the proceedings are being filmed, it's probably best to remain seated during the question and answer period. This saves the people operating cameras the bother of having to constantly adjust their lenses.

Panels at press conferences are always fearful that people either will not turn up or, if they do, will not ask any questions. The most common reasons for an initial lack of questions are either the fear that a query will expose lack of concentration or because a journalist doesn't want to reveal the angle of his story. The rhetorical question is a good ploy to get things going:

> The question that seems to be on everybody's lips at the moment is . . .

Alternatively, have a couple of 'plants' (colleagues) in the audience who are ready with a prepared question should they need to ask it. If you're in the Chair, it's very important that you 'lead from the front'. You must let your audience know which questioner you'll be going to next, how much time has elapsed and how many questions may still be asked.

An important point for your panel to remember throughout a press conference is that it is as vital to *listen* attentively as it is to *talk* engagingly. It is all too easy, while a colleague is performing, to 'switch off' and start planning next year's holiday. Lack of concentration usually manifests itself visibly as extreme boredom or deep depression. Don't underestimate the difficulty of looking interested. Natural inhibition will tend to suppress silent gestures of encouragement, but you must not allow it to do so. However unnatural you may feel, if you do make a concerted effort to look at the speaker, nod in agreement, smile at his or her humorous remarks (even if you heard them last week at the office party) both the speaker and your audience will be with you.

Press conferences, just like interviews, are all about taking and keeping *control*. One effective way of asserting yourself is to listen to a question, interpret it as if you're repeating it, and then give your reply. Don't be afraid of a supplementary from a questioner, but never forget that you're the one in charge and, if you feel the time is right to move on, then do so. Don't be surprised if a journalist tries to draw you on a subject which you don't think is relevant to the conference. It's a ruse often tried on politicians. Firmly, but politely, remind the conference that you are there to talk about 'x' but not 'y'.

As the time for questions and answers draws to a close, use the final moments to recap on the *three* important things you want to say. You may be lucky and hit upon an indolent journalist or two who are only too grateful not to have to go back through their notes, or whose memories will be effectively jogged by the recap.

Light refreshments and the informal press conference

Just because people in the media believe *they* can think and drink at the same time, don't for one moment forget the cardinal rule – *no alcohol until the party's over*. If it's important that you *seem* to be imbibing, have a glass of wine and a mineral water beside you. No one will notice that you're only drinking the non-alcoholic one.

Whether you decide to offer your guests a full meal or a buffet after the press conference, always make sure there are

enough seats and also quiet corners where individual interviews can be conducted.

Although post-press conference gatherings tend to be less
stressful than the formal presentation, never forget that it is
still a *public* function and that anything you say is 'on the
record'. This is the time when journalists will want to pursue
their individual angles on the story. Be as helpful as you can,
but remember that your rights still apply (see p. 71). If there
is something you can't answer, then don't attempt to do so.
Either promise to get back to them later, or divert them with
some other information.

The press briefing

Press briefings seem to be gaining in popularity,
perhaps because the instigator feels able to exercise
more control over two or three people than over a
rabble. Certainly they tend to be less formal, usually taking
place over a drink or a meal, and seeming to have a less defined
structure. To avoid the competitive element, don't ask four
features editors from four national papers to join you for breakfast. Far better to vary the mix by bringing together people
from a daily paper, a monthly magazine, a trade publication
and a local paper. This will give each journalist the opportunity
to pursue his or her own angle without fear of duplication.
However, just because the atmosphere may be more informal,
never forget that you're 'on the record' and that there must
be no indiscretions.

'Off the record' – fact or fiction?

My first job in television was as a researcher/writer for *This is
Your Life*. We were a small, closely knit team and, not surprisingly, I got to know Eamonn Andrews well.

On one occasion, when a colleague phoned me asking for a
'bit of background' to help him with a profile he was writing for

the *TV Times*, I naively assumed that the colourful descriptions I began giving of Mr Andrews were just 'background'. Summoned to the Producer's office two days later, I learnt a valuable, if painful, lesson. My indiscretions shrieked off the page of the *TV Times*, made worse by being attributed. And I only had myself to blame.

There is no such thing as 'off the record'. If you don't want it recorded, don't say it.

There are, however, some exceptions. Joan Thirkettle of ITN says:

> If I didn't have 'off the record' conversations, it would be hard to get at the true facts of a story in the short time we have to put an item together. For instance, if I'm covering a story about a government report to be published at 1 p.m. that day, and I have to get the story ready for the one o'clock news, I would ring my contact at the relevant government department, explain the situation and ask for guidance, i.e. prior knowledge of what the report contains, on the understanding that the embargo would not be broken.

And Graham Lancaster of Biss Lancaster makes the following comment:

> If you are not experienced in dealing with the press, I would never advise anyone to go off the record but, speaking as a professional, I find it a useful device, either to stop a story running, or broaden the journalist's understanding of the issue, thereby increasing my chances of being represented sympathetically.
>
> The 'off the record' quote is still used, with some degree of success, in political circles. When you read the preamble, 'a government spokesman said' or 'an industry source tells me', you can be pretty sure that a journalist has persuaded someone to divulge some sensitive information on the basis that it remains non-attributable.

49

The follow-up

If you've obeyed the rules in this chapter, picking up the papers the morning after your press conference could come as a pleasant surprise.

If you have been accurately and fairly reported, take the trouble to write and thank the journalist. Conversely, if there are any errors or any gross distortions of the truth, you have to decide what, if any, action you will take. How to complain is dealt with in Chapter 7.

Remember

- Consider carefully when to hold a press conference.
- Choose the venue with care, and try to insist on rehearsal time.
- Be selective with your visual aids and make sure you know how to use them and that they work.
- Presentation is all – provide information packs.
- The first 30 seconds of your opening remarks must be made without notes.
- Don't forget to smile.
- Use the windscreen wiper technique to maintain audience eye contact.
- To err is human. Don't allow a mistake during delivery to unhinge you. Smile, apologize and carry on.
- Use gesture to enhance your performance.
- Vary the pitch and pace of your voice, and use pauses for dramatic effect.
- Keep a firm grip on the question and answer session and let the audience know when time is running out.
- Always make sure you know who is asking a question.
- Put as much effort into listening as you do into speaking.
- Nothing during a press conference is off the record.
- Never drink alcohol.
- Speaking in public is a performance. Failure to treat it as such will seriously diminish the impact of your speech.

PART TWO
MARRIAGE

3 How to prepare for an interview

A well-known military axiom which has proved its worth over the centuries is just as appropriate as regards the media:

Time spent on reconnaissance is seldom wasted.

You have only to substitute 'research' for 'reconnaissance' to have a piece of invaluable advice for a prospective media interview.

Unless you know what *you* want to say, you will never be able to *take control*, which is the ultimate goal of any interviewee. And don't think you can mug it up at the last minute. You *can't*. Anyone who anticipates at some stage coming into media contact should, just like Baden-Powell's young Scouts, 'be prepared'. Try carrying with you a small mental attaché case containing up-to-date company statistics, personal anecdotes and plans for the future. Such endeavour *always* pays off because, whatever the line of questioning, you will *never* be at a loss for words.

Do I really want this interview?

It was the late Andy Warhol who claimed that 'In the future, everyone will be famous for fifteen minutes', and there's no denying the initial flurry of conceit when a press call comes through. But unfortunately, even those at ease with the media will inevitably inflate the importance of that call. Of course it is and should be important to *you*, but to the rest of the world your news is fleeting and probably of limited interest.

53

If that is the case, why don't I stop reading this book and return to my ostrich-like refusal to admit the existence of the media? Because if you do decide to go ahead, you're exposing yourself to the possibility of winning free airtime or column inches to promote your ideas or product.

Just as agony aunts in popular magazines advise the 'debit and credit' technique to help the emotionally indecisive, so you should draw up a balance sheet to help you decide whether or not to talk to the media.

Positive	Negative
1 It's an opportunity for free publicity.	It could backfire.
2 Editorial coverage adds objective credibility.	They may not get the message right.
3 Talking to the press can put a stop to rumours.	Talking to the press can inflame rumours.
4 You can put the record straight.	By so doing, you may betray professional confidences.
5 You could well be asked back.	You could fall flat on your face.

An immediate appraisal doesn't lead to an obvious choice. There seems to be as much against embracing the media as there does for avoiding it. Except for one vital factor: if you prepare rigorously, the five negatives are far less likely to win against the five positives.

There is, of course, no law that says you *have* to talk, but you are more likely to have some control over the situation if you accept than if you decline an invitation to participate. We all know what we think when we hear the oft-repeated phrase, 'We asked Trip-Up & Co. for their opinion, but they declined to comment'. Trip-Up & Co. may have a spotless record, but one 'and they refused to comment' on the local television news and their honesty rating plummets.

There will be occasions when it will be imprudent to talk (during a merger or takeover, for instance), in which case you have to learn to deflect the enquiries without incurring the media's disparagement.

Honesty is often a useful ally in this situation:

> I wish I could answer that question personally, but you're actually talking to the wrong person. You really should contact so-and-so.

If the reporter is determined, he or she may well try and make contact with 'so-and-so', so please remember to notify your colleague. Although you are referring the query in all honesty to someone more appropriate, because of the journalist's deadline you may have deterred him or her by default and so achieved a breathing space.

You can also try this ploy – again, often based on truth:

> I *would* like to talk on your programme, but can you save it for a couple of weeks? As I'm sure you'll appreciate, we're in the middle of our stock-taking period, and we're up against our own deadlines. If you could ring me back after the 20th, I'd be more than happy to talk with you.

This apparently helpful reply should have conveyed several messages to the reporter:

1 You're not averse to talking on the programme.
2 You and he are in the same boat as far as 'deadlines' are concerned.
3 You'll more than amply repay the implied debt by giving the reporter what he wants (and more) at a later date.

As a final resort, you might try taking the journalist into your confidence and explain 'off the record' why you're unable at that particular time to participate in the interview. This is an option which should be exercised only with extreme caution. There is already a sufficient element of gambling in media communication without deliberately stacking the odds against yourself.

Let us assume that you have opted for the *positive* route and are about to submit yourself to the mercy of the media.

Types of interview

Interviews fall roughly into three categories:

- information seeking
- expert opinion
- gladiatorial

Information seeking

Most interviews fall into this category. The reporter acts as a conduit for your thoughts. Although he or she may elaborately disguise the fact, there are only six basic questions: who, what, when, why, where and how.

Expert opinion

There are rich pickings to be had from those who can persuade a newspaper or a television or radio station that they have specialist knowledge. The reporter merely has to press the 'on' switch and let you inform and entertain the audience. Not only will you be unlikely to get hostile questions – the interviewer wouldn't have the gall to give you a hard time, as you are giving him or her such an easy one – but you will be holding centre stage and will have numerous opportunities to mention your own company. The local media, especially, welcome expert opinions, and it's worth cultivating key contacts to make sure that, when a situation arises, you're the one they phone for a comment.

Gladiatorial

As its title suggests, this is potentially the most hazardous type of interview with which you'll be confronted. And, to make matters worse, it will usually happen at a time when you least want it. Just as any Chancellor of the Exchequer cannot relish the periodic publication of the trade figures, nor might you wish to have the spotlight turned on your company's announced redundancy plans. In this situation, the reporter will inevitably take the self-righteous attitude of protecting the country's employment, making it very difficult for you to turn the interview to your positive advantage. But you can, and you will.

Types of interviewer

Just as there are types of interview, so there are types of interviewer.

Aggressive

One of the media's favourite ways of introducing an item is to conduct what is known as a 'vox pop', an abbreviation of the Latin *vox populi*, voice of the people. Men and women are selected at random, usually in a busy shopping street, and asked their opinions on anything from nuclear disarmament to wife-swapping. My own vox pop, conducted to find the country's most aggressive interviewer, yielded the unanimous response 'Sir Robin Day', whose imperious manner towards bores and dissemblers made him world famous.

One of his well-remembered encounters was during the 1982 Conservative Party conference. As he describes in his book *Grand Inquisitor*, the Rt Hon. John Nott, then Secretary of State for Defence, had been addressing the party that day at Brighton. As this was the first conference since the Falklands War, the media was no doubt waiting to see what, if any, reference would be made to it. When Nott came into the BBC's location studio to record his interview for the early evening *Nationwide* programme, Robin Day pressed home the observation that numerous critical conference resolutions about naval policy had not been debated by the conference. Obviously irritated by the persistent jibes, Nott retorted:

It really does not do the integrity of the services much good if respected people like you seek to draw divisions between ministers and chiefs of staff. This is damaging to the services.

As if determined to pierce the politician's armour, Robin Day continued with a penetrating line of questions. Did Mr Nott regard his now cancelled decision to sell HMS *Invincible* as an error of judgement? Then came the final twist of the knife. Referring to the fact that Nott had recently announced his retirement from Parliament at the forthcoming election, Day asked:

Why should the public on this issue believe you, a transient, here today and, if I may say so, gone tomorrow politician, rather than a senior officer of many years' experience?

Nott tore the microphone from his lapel and threw it on the table saying:

I'm sorry – I am fed up with this interview. It is ridiculous.

This incident shows only too clearly the perils of allowing oneself to be unsettled by such a 'gladiator' as Sir Robin Day. Although our sympathies usually lie with the 'victim' of this type of interview, the fact that Nott walked out meant that he missed a valuable opportunity to put the government's view.

When faced with an aggressive interviewer, the first rule is never to allow yourself to be provoked into over-reacting.

A while ago, when Robin Day published his memoirs, I was given the opportunity to turn the tables and interview *him*. Is this a case of aggressor turned aggressee?

As he called his memoirs *Sir Robin Day – Grand Inquisitor*, I first asked him if that was how he saw himself.

Not particularly, no, but the word 'grand inquisitor' has appeared dozens of times in newspaper articles and profiles for the past twenty years or so, and the publishers and I thought it was a better title than most of the boring puns on the word 'day'.

So you believe what you read in the press?

No, I don't believe what I read in the press. It was a title which had already been used about me.

What surprises me about your memoirs is that they are far less acerbic than I expected them to be. They are much softer, and I wondered, therefore, if we have the aggressive, forthright Sir Robin Day on television, but if I met you at a dinner party, you would be quite different?

Well, you mustn't believe everything you see on television. In the first place I can't imagine why you expected something acerbic and aggressive if you have seen me regularly on television because most people who have seen me regularly on television think I am rather good humoured, tolerant and rather patient. I don't know if you ever saw me interviewing the Prime Minister or Mr Kinnock ...

I certainly have ...

Then you must have gone down on your knees and thanked God for somebody so patient, good tempered and good humoured as poor old Robin Day.

But I have also seen you interview Sir John Nott and get him so excited and so distressed that he walked out of the interview.

That is the only occasion it has happened and it was only a two-minute interview and I don't know why he did it; nor do one or two of his cabinet colleagues.

Do you see yourself as a champion for the people?

No, I just see myself as a humble servant of democracy, one of many appointed to seek the truth.

Who enjoys the publicity, who enjoys being recognized, who enjoys being caricatured in newspapers?

Are you asking me a question or making a series of statements?

There is a question mark in my voice.

To me it was one of those questions which had been answered before it was posed.

Do you enjoy being in the limelight?

I would not enjoy being in darkness if I had been on television for thirty-five years. But as my poor old friend Ludovic Kennedy said to me in an interview the other night. He said to me, 'Do you enjoy being impersonated? Nobody tried to impersonate me in 35 years, does that make me a dull dog?' I said, 'Well, you must draw your own conclusions.'

Sir Robin Day signed my copy of the book, 'For Miss Sarah Dickinson, with warm regards from her *humblest* interviewee.'

Ill-informed

A prolific breed this one, particularly encountered by authors on tour, being interviewed by 'jocks' who have only read the blurb on the jacket. Before coming to interview you, or you joining them, they will have spent five minutes in the cuttings library, usually looking at the two most recent cuttings and a couple of older ones. Whilst involved in their rapid fami- liarization course, they tend to forget that they are the journal- ists and shouldn't take the printed word as proven fact. If there's an error in one of the top cuttings, it will be perpetuated in the interview.

You must be prepared not only for questions based on erroneous information from an ill-informed reporter, but also for sweepingly general ones. The most dreaded question to a novelist is:

What's your book about?

To the historian:

In a sentence, why do you think America invaded Vietnam?

To the politician:

Yes or no?

Opinionated

Scratch the surface of an opinionated interviewer and, likely as not, you'll find an expert *manqué* or school teacher. On many occasions, their questions are longer than your answers, they litter them with the names of the good and the famous, and often burnish the performance with obscure quotes from the forgotten poets:

> It's hard, when seeing your situation in relation to those who would have been your contemporaries in the eighteenth century, not to be reminded of Dante's final stanza in his poem ...

We do eventually get to a question but, by the time we do, your intellectual confidence has been reduced to rubble and 99 per cent of the audience has been lost.

Unctuous

Every newspaper, or television or radio station has an unctuous interviewer. Their powers are lethal. They will cajole, flatter and amuse you right to the second before the 'on air' light turns from green to red. Lulled into a false sense of security, you will be shocked and distracted by the swift and unexpected change in tone. As Hamlet said, 'One may smile, and smile, and be a villain.'

Bored

It is unrealistic to expect reporters to show a universal interest in all subjects. Unfortunately, some disguise the fact less well than others. It is most disconcerting to discover that *your* export drive on metal flanges doesn't seem to arouse a reporter as much as it does yourself, and even more galling when he manifests his lack of interest by flirting with the female studio engineer or conducting a conversation with the producer.

As will become clear in Chapter 5, there are some very simple rules for dealing with *all* types of interviewer.

Research your audience

Now that we've grasped how to avoid a reporter if we
don't want to make a comment, and how to recognize
certain types if we do, we are almost ready to begin
the serious preparation.

You wouldn't turn up to a business presentation in a satin
tutu, so you shouldn't dream of talking to a journalist or
appearing on a radio or television programme without first
establishing the 'mental mode of dress'. Is it a jeans and sweater
type of show or more formal? Take the trouble to listen to the
programme, video a show or read a journalist's copy. And take
your cue from them. Television presenter Selina Scott takes
her cue from you or me:

> I don't really have an image of myself that I want to project.
> Clothes are part of the business, part of the system. I put myself
> in other people's places. If I am going to do an interview with
> someone who is quite shy about it, I will wear something which
> will not overwhelm them in colour or style.
> (*Sunday Times*, 22 October 1989)

Just as Selina adjusts her wardrobe depending on whom she
is to interview, so you will temper the style of your interviews
depending on the programme or publication. (You will also
carefully choose what you wear, but that will be discussed in
Chapter 5.) Because you've monitored the various programmes
and read the relevant newspapers and magazines, you will
know, before you're asked to perform, the style of your outlet.
If it's the *Jimmy Young Programme*, you know you've got to be
cosily informative – no long words, no jargon and *no aggression*.
If, on the other hand, you've got two and a half minutes on
BBC Radio 4's *Today* programme, you know that you will have
to be much more succinct.

Researching your audience not only gives you a valuable
headstart over your interviewer (remember we said how lax
most reporters are when it comes to research), but you'll also
find that a little bit of flattery goes a *very* long way. I speak for

all gullible journalists. An interviewee only has to walk into my studio, grip me firmly by the hand, look directly into my eyes and utter the immortal phrase, 'I did so enjoy your show last night', and I am to do with as he or she wills. The irony is that it doesn't even seem to matter if I suspect they're lying. The evidence of effort to flatter is sufficient to make me withdraw the claws.

Prepare your arguments

Until you know what *you* want to get out of an interview, you will seldom be satisfied by the way you come across. Most of us, because we haven't sorted our thoughts before meeting the press, fall into the trap of trying to tell the *whole* story. You, because of the stress of the situation, will inevitably lose your train of thought. Result – bad communication all round.

Always think in threes. Let's suppose you've been invited to join your local radio breakfast show to talk about the extension to your factory to be opened by the Lord Mayor that afternoon. You've listened to the programme for a couple of days, so you know its style and the presenters' names. You'll know how long each item tends to last and you'll have made sure you know the whereabouts of the radio station.

You now take a piece of paper and write down all the *positive* things you want to say about the factory extension – the list should come to at least ten points. This will be seven too many. Now you become your own editor. Which *three* points are the ones you're going to make on that radio show, or to that local newspaper reporter? It is almost arbitrary which three you choose – the important thing to remember is that it *must be only three*.

Why three should be the key number to memory retention is as questionable as why we prefer reading bad rather than good news. But when it comes to making a point forcefully, the triple approach is always the most effective. Neil Kinnock, leader of the Labour Party:

> We are in the lead. We are going to sustain our lead. We are going to win our election.
> (*Sunday Correspondent*, 1 October 1989)

President Bush on the purge of drug dealers:

> They will be caught, prosecuted, punished.
> (Television broadcast, 5 September 1989)

A local vicar at a christening urged his congregation to:

> Believe, belong, continue.

Lord Reith, founder of the BBC, believed it had a duty to:

> Educate, inform and entertain.

Depending on your audience, the choice of the particular three points will invariably change. If you're new to the media game, a useful starting point is to make sure one of your three points is your company's name. You'd be surprised at the number of people who give excellent interviews on behalf of their industry as a whole, forgetting completely to identify themselves. Unlike Americans, for whom self-promotion seems second nature, the British have to learn to shed their diffidence. A useful rule is to bring in the company name early in the interview:

> We at Tip-Top have always been proud of our industrial record ...

This not only relieves you of the burden of trying to remember to introduce the company name later, but also gives you the opportunity to link it with something positive.

However, you have to be careful not to *overstate* either your company or its wares. As a general rule, broadcasters usually credit you and your company in the introduction to the piece and in the back-announcement. You risk their ire and subsequent verbal put-down if you've been too liberal with the plugs during the interview.

A question often asked by pupils of media training sessions, and rightly so, is how can the three points be made in response to questions that appear to have no bearing on the subject? Chapter 5 deals with this conundrum.

Once the three *key* points have been isolated, you should refer back to the remaining seven on the list. Three *additional* positive points will stand you in good stead when dealing with the inevitable supplementary questions.

So, how far have we got in preparation for a media encounter? We've researched our audience and have decided upon a particular tone to our interview. We've listened to or watched our programme, or familiarized ourselves with the relevant publication. We are confident in the three points that we intend to make. In theory, we should be more than adequately prepared.

Except for one remaining strand – *the negatives.*

Just as the 'pending' tray seems to be the one always overlooked in the office filing system, so the 'negative' recess of the brain is the one to which we give least attention. None of us likes admitting that something is not as it should be, but if you are going to win in the media stakes, you *must* face up to the negatives, if only for the obvious reason that, if questioned about them, you will stutter and stumble and lose control of the interview. For instance, if you know that your interim figures are down on last year, be ready to deal with a question challenging you on your competence. Because your inquisitor is probably poorly briefed about you and your company, the question may never arise, but imagine your public discomfort if he or she does raise the subject and you're unable to deal with it.

More disconcerting than not being able to deal with a negative question is the terrifying experience of hearing *yourself* involuntarily introducing a negative into your answer. It always strikes me that there are three serious biological design faults in the human body.

- We always grin into a camera, even in moments of extreme stress.
- The mouth dries and the palms sweat just before we go 'on air'.
- The brain seems sometimes to deliberately sabotage any

attempt to appear half-way competent by making us say something totally inappropriate to the moment.

A classic case in point was during a typical media training seminar I conducted recently. Three senior hotel executives from a major chain had been sent to us to learn about dealing with the media and, in particular, about how to deal with a crisis.

There are three potential crisis areas for hoteliers:

- fire
- food poisoning
- an accident

Having explained to my three trainees, who were already quaking in anticipation of the quizzing to come, that I was going to take each of them in turn and conduct what is referred to as a 'door stepping' interview, I gave them the brief scenario of fourteen of their hotel guests being rushed to hospital with suspected salmonella poisoning.

Trainee number one was unceremoniously directed into a corridor where he was greeted by a crew, one with a hand-held light and large microphone, one with a camera on his shoulder, and an interviewer.

Interviewer: We've just heard, Mr Jeeves, that fourteen of your guests have been rushed to hospital with salmonella poisoning. [Note the implied statement in the question.]

Mr Jeeves: [who begins well] We don't know that it *was* salmonella poisoning ...

The interviewer employs the oldest trick in the book and stares at the interviewee purposefully, willing him to continue, which he obligingly does.

Mr Jeeves: Yes, it could have perhaps been an air-borne disease ...

There is no hope for Mr Jeeves – he has dug his grave and the interviewer is going to let him lie in it.

Mr Jeeves: ... something like legionnaires' disease.

Not only had Mr Jeeves committed his hotel chain to an entire overhaul of their air-conditioning units, he had committed every conceivable error in dealing with a crisis interview (dealt with separately in Chapter 6). And mainly because he hadn't sufficiently prepared himself for dealing with a possible question about legionnaires' disease, he found *himself* rather than the interviewer introducing the controversial subject.

On a potentially less damaging scale, ill-prepared interviewees will often, again unconsciously, introduce either a negative train of thought into an answer, or simply an inappropriate adjective. Be wary of so doing. Journalists may not be well researched, but they are very alert to anything out of the ordinary and, at the merest suggestion of stress, prevarication or discomfort, will jettison their planned list of questions and go for the jugular:

Q: What was your turnover last year?

A: I think it was in the region of £200 million.

Q: Is that a satisfactory result?

A: Well, we're reasonably pleased with it, yes.

Q: Only reasonably – you seem to be suggesting that you should have done better ...

The word 'reasonable' may be quite acceptable in the accounting world, but to a journalist it spells disappointment, which indicates the beginning of a negative story.

How to anticipate questions

 For an inexperienced interviewee, the prospect of trying to anticipate interviewers' questions is always a daunting one. How are you supposed to read their fevered minds? You don't have to. Simply remember that, however much they may dress the set, there are very few basic questions: who, what, why, when, where and how?

There is absolutely no point in trying to play mental chess *during* an interview – you will never be able to cope with answering the interviewer's questions, trying to take control *and* guessing the interviewer's next move. But it will pay dividends to do so beforehand.

Make a list of all the questions you'd most *like* to be asked and prepare your answers, imagining possible supplementaries. You will be surprised how closely the interviewer seems to be following your script. Also make a list of those questions you hope *won't* be raised. And again, draw up prepared answers. Such preparation won't give you total protection as interviewers, like humans, are often unpredictable, but it will certainly help.

Handling interviewers' tricks

What is more of a skil' is being able to deal with some of the tricks employed by interviewers to try and make you say more than you probably should.

Pregnant pause

We have just seen this used to great effect in the salmonella poisoning interview. By the interviewer's refusal to ask the next question, the interviewee feels compelled to fill the 'dead' airtime and, as a result, goes on to say things best left unsaid.

The pregnant pause is easily and effectively dealt with by being firm, but tactful:

> I don't think I can add anything further on that point. What is interesting, however, is ...

This seemingly innocuous reply has not only succeeded in stopping the interviewer's persistent line of questioning, but taken the initiative and put you in *control*.

Promise of performance

There are occasions when an interviewer, just before you go on air, will tell you how he or she is going to start the interview. This declaration has the immediate effect of putting you at your ease and giving you a chance momentarily to prepare your first answer. *Very* occasionally, you'll come up against a less principled interviewer who, having told you how he or she intends to start, will actually begin with a completely different question.

This is shabby behaviour and, for the inexperienced, can be very unnerving. There are two ways to deal with it. Either tell your audience that this wasn't the question you'd been told to expect, but you'll have a go at answering it, or don't let on that you've been misled and answer the question to the best of your ability. The fact that you will have done your homework and the interviewer probably won't have will be of great help in this situation.

Loaded introduction

Some interviewers will take every opportunity to show off, and an obvious place for a display of verbal vanity is in their introduction. They may have only approximately 30 seconds, but that is often quite long enough to give a totally misleading impression of the item to come. Always *listen closely* to an introduction and have the courage to correct it if you feel it's sufficiently important so to do.

Leading question

It is said that the truly great interviewer is the one whom the audience doesn't notice. If the converse is true, the interviewer who posits a fact *and* expresses an opinion is a bad one. But that knowledge doesn't necessarily make it any easier to deal with a leading question: 'So, basically, your *only* motivation was profit?' or 'If we look at your track record on recycling, we'll see that your "green" policy is rather weak ...'

69

The way to handle questions such as these will be dealt with in Chapter 5.

Incomprehensible question

Many questions will be incomprehensible. It matters not. So long as you don't insult your interviewer by highlighting his or her muddled thoughts, seize the initiative and take from the question what you will.

Open question

This is a favourite reporter's ruse. The interviewer will appear, in the most reasonable manner, to present you with a series of questions posed almost as a statement. Again, you are not obliged to try and unravel the interviewer's prejudices, so merely use it as a springboard for your opinions.

The authenticity of the story surrounding former Labour Prime Minister Lord Wilson's treatment of his interviewers in the BBC *Panorama* studio is debatable. But it is alleged that, whenever he arrived for interview, he would hand a sheaf of notes to the presenter with a crisp 'There are my answers. What are your questions?'

Like most politicians, Harold Wilson was a prime exponent of the 'you never have to answer a question' school of interviewees. Many of my media trainees are anxious that, once they've mastered the skills of being in control of the interview, they will all sound as slippery and insincere as most of our politicians. I am happy to report that this so-called skill takes *years* of *daily* practice to acquire.

Winding-down question

Most honourable journalists will let you know when an interview is coming to an end and mean it. Some, however, will use it as a device to lull you into a false sense of security:

One final question, when do you see your company going on to the USM?

You answer the question to the best of your ability, and begin to think of taking your leave, only to be brought abruptly to attention by a barked:

> So, you think shareholders would be interested in a company that made forty people redundant last year?

It might be below the belt, but it was your fault. You shouldn't have assumed the interview was over until the microphone was switched off.

An interviewee's rights

Over the years, the media have come to accept that, if an interview is to be half-way fair and half-way interesting, then the interviewee *must* be afforded certain basic rights. (The IBA publishes programme guidelines, a tradition which will probably be continued by the newly formed Independent Television Commission and Radio Authority.)

Unfortunately, very few people in the media ever take the trouble to tell the interviewee what some of those rights are. This is not because they are being deliberately deceitful; it is simply because common courtesies tend to get overlooked in the frenzy of a radio or television studio.

However stressful you might find the environment, it is in *your* interests to assert *your* rights. To do so inevitably leads to you rather than they being in control. But a word of warning. It is *very* unwise to use this inside knowledge as a vehicle for authority. You know and we know, so let's leave it at that. An interviewee who clumsily insists on asserting his rights at every stage of an interview will not be popular and will almost certainly never be asked back.

You have the right to know:

- the title and style of the programme on which you've been asked to appear;
- whether the interview is to be live or recorded;

- how long your spot will be;
- the *broad* outline of the interview;
- whether it will be 'one-to-one' interview or a group discussion;
- the interviewer's first question;
- when the programme will be transmitted;
- how you will be credited.

You also have the right:

- to go back and correct something, even if the programme has been recorded;
- not to talk to a journalist who gets through to you without prior warning.

You do *not* have a right to:

- see a transcript or copy of a programme before it is transmitted, or ask for an audio or video copy afterwards;
- demand a detailed list of the questions prior to the interview;
- insist on not being asked certain questions;
- decide where you want to appear in the running order of any particular programme.

Title and style of programme

Being intensely arrogant creatures, television and radio producers will automatically assume that you are a devoted fan of their programme, and they may not, therefore, tell you enough about it. It is in *your* interest that you ask. What is the programme? Is it part of a series? When is it transmitted? Is it repeated? How many people watch?

As I will be at pains to point out throughout this book, an encounter with a media person must always be regarded, as far as is humanly possible, as a two-way relationship. In other words, just as it is in your interest to establish some basic facts about a programme before deciding whether or not to participate, so it is the duty of the producer or researcher to make sure that he or she knows who you are.

Several years ago, in the early days of LBC (London's first

all-talk independent commercial radio station) when the ubiquitous phone-in was the easiest and cheapest way of filling airtime, Richard Holmes, then Chairman of the Liberal Party, was invited to join the station for an hour-long phone-in. Mr Holmes assumed that the subject under discussion would be the state of the Liberal Party, so we can imagine his surprise when he heard himself being introduced as Richard Hope, Editor of *Railway Gazette*, invited on to the programme to give his views on the state of British Rail.

Researchers are fallible and any of us could have made the same mistake. In LBC's card index, Holmes was probably pretty close to Hope. Had it not been for Holmes' political talent – an accomplished facility for opportunism – LBC would have had one very embarrassed producer on its hands.

Live and recorded interviews

The only sure way of knowing that you won't be misquoted or taken out of context is always to appear *live*. Politicians such as Tony Benn insist upon it, but most of us will not be able to exert that kind of authority. The important thing to remember is always to *ask beforehand*. If in doubt, always assume it's live, which will prevent you from committing the verbal blunders that we've all heard others make:

You're not going to ask about ... are you?

or, even more amateur:

Are we on?

The *advantages* of doing a recorded interview are:

● You have the opportunity to re-record the interview if you are unhappy with your performance. Editing is a very fast and simple process in radio. Magnetic tape is cut with a razor blade and spliced with good old-fashioned sticky tape. It can be remarkably accurate. Sound, for radio, is always recorded at either $7\frac{1}{2}$ or 15 inches per second, so you can imagine how much tape one stumbling 'errr' occupies. Television editing can be almost as accurate, but it is a much more costly procedure, involving the use of complex video editing machines. You will find, as a rule, that a television producer would rather re-record an entire section than go to the expense of complicated and costly editing.

● The recorded interview tends to be less stressful and less formal than a live one, which should give you the chance to establish a warmer bond with the interviewer.

● There is always a much longer 'warm-up' period prior to recording an interview, which gives you the chance to indulge in some crafty auto-suggestion:

I don't know whether you saw the latest Work for Women agency report which came out this morning. It makes fascinating reading. Seventy-five per cent of the young women interviewed said they intended to combine a career with a family.

Don't be surprised to hear the interviewer immediately assume authorship of this information and use it in the introduction (the cue):

According to a survey published today by the Work for Women agency, 75 per cent of the young women interviewed . . .

By taking the initiative, you have not only demonstrated your ability to be in *control*, but also ensured that your organisation is mentioned by the interviewer.

The *disadvantage* of doing a recorded interview is that, once you've left a radio or television studio, you've essentially relinquished any editorial rights over the piece. Of course, if a malicious editor makes you appear to say something completely opposite to your actual statement, there is redress. But it is very rarely that someone's speech is so drastically distorted as to warrant a public correction. What tends to happen is that your view as to what is relevant or interesting may not coincide with the editor's. Result – what you consider to have been pearls of wisdom end up on the cutting room floor, and your unintentional gaffs are given alarming prominence. Chapter 5 will deal with how to avoid such pitfalls.

Length of spot

You must assert the right to know not only how much of your time is required overall, but also how long you will actually be 'on air'. If you're going to appear on a phone-in, you could get an hour or more. If, on the other hand, you've been invited to appear on the *Today* programme, you'll be lucky to get more than three minutes. Establishing your time allocation should be an *essential* part of your research.

Broad outline of interview

As I said, you do *not* have a right to see a detailed list of questions before going into an interview. The pompous always give the excuse of not wanting to spoil the spontaneity of the conversation. Closer to the truth would be the ill-preparedness of the interviewer.

But you *do* have a right to know the particular angle a producer intends to take with an item.

Supposing you represent the oil industry. Before going any-where near a programme like BBC's *Newsnight* – known to savage the most experienced verbal warriors – you would establish the parameters. Will the programme be looking at oil and the environment or oil as an essential part of the Middle Eastern economy? Don't blame the interviewer if you find yourself on the skid-pan because you failed to exercise so fundamental a right.

One-to-one interviews and group discussions

Why is it that consenting adults, used to asking pertinent questions, change into dumb supplicants when approached by the media? You may not wish to take part in an interview with a competitor – especially if you know that he or she is more articulate. Far better that you are able to make that choice *before* getting into the studio and finding yourself pre-sented with a *fait accompli*.

In 1986, at the height of the Westland Affair, the Rt Hon. Michael Heseltine caused almost as much of a stir as when he lifted the Mace from its hallowed resting place in the House of Commons and swirled it above his head. For some weeks the row had been raging over the future ownership of the defence manufacturing company Westland. Heseltine, frustrated by the Government's handling of the matter, walked out of a cabinet meeting at No. 10 Downing Street, and announced his resignation as Secretary of State for Defence.

The media can't resist a resignation, especially of someone as striking as Michael Heseltine. Within minutes of his announcement, he began a tour of the news stations, and at 7 p.m. it was the turn of *Channel 4 News*, hosted by Peter Sissons.

As regular viewers of news programmes will know, the presenter always begins the bulletin with a short list of the forthcoming news items – known in the media as 'the menu'. Peter Sissons began this particular broadcast, not surprisingly, with the news of the Defence Secretary's resignation. A little further down his contents list, he came to the anticipated arrival of Clive Ponting, the former civil servant who was acquitted of breaking the Official Secrets Act by leaking documents about the sinking of the Argentine cruiser, *General Belgrano*. As Michael Heseltine could well be seen as the loser in this particular nail-biting confrontation, he was not at all pleased to learn of Mr Ponting's impending presence:

> Nobody told me about this. You don't expect me to appear on a programme with Clive Ponting. You don't expect me to treat him as a serious civil servant.
>
> (*Daily Mail*, 17 January 1986)

So saying, he swept out of the studio.

It made riveting television but, like John Nott in the Robin Day interview, by losing *control*, Heseltine almost missed a valuable opportunity to get his message across to *exactly* the audience he was trying to woo. In fact, Heseltine was lucky. Being who he is, he managed to get Ponting's appearance delayed until the next day, and then returned ten minutes later to be interviewed. You may not be so lucky. I suspect that, in this situation, no one from Heseltine's office had taken the precaution of ringing the Channel 4 news room to try and establish a list of news stories, or had attempted to put themselves in the producer's shoes in order to anticipate what googlies would be bowled at the minister.

It is a sad fact that the media are often underhand when it comes to involving you in programme content. TV coverage of a firework story one year was a classic example of an inexperienced interviewee falling into a tried and tested trap.

A firework manufacturer had agreed to take part in what he thought was an interview about firework safety. Imagine his consternation when his live studio interview was prefaced by an emotive film about children being killed by fireworks. He was far too inexperienced even to attempt to salvage the situation, and probably has avoided all contact with the media since.

The lesson to be learnt from this incident is *always to ask* and *never to trust*. You have been warned.

The interviewer's first question

Precisely what to expect when you get to a television or radio studio will be outlined in Chapter 4. What you certainly *can't* expect is interviewers to automatically tell you what their first question is going to be. But you have the right to ask and, more than likely if you do, they'll tell you.

Remember, again, that a successful interview has to be interactive. It's as much in the interviewer's interests to get you off to a confident start as it is in yours. Listeners and viewers are intolerant people who will switch channels at the first hint of uncertainty, so both of you must do your best to avoid this happening.

As in all delicate encounters, tact is of the essence. It won't get you anywhere to throw down the gauntlet and demand to know the first question; the reporter will smell a media-trained rat immediately. Far more effective to use a phrase like 'How do you intend to begin the interview?' or 'Any idea how you'll start?'

You would be more than justified at this point to wonder if the media likes its interviewees to arrive bristling with media techniques. On the whole, so long as the knowledge is not too obvious, it does. It is ironic that, despite the obvious advantage of experience and home territory, the interviewer is often only as good as the interviewee. I know from my own experience that I conduct a much more spirited interview with a pacey, lively interviewee than with a halting, underconfident one.

Programme transmission

So grateful are most of us to have seemed to survive our media ordeal that simple enquiries, such as when the programme will be transmitted or the article printed, fly from our minds. It is important that you ask, if only to give yourself time to arrange for recordings and to alert prospective clients. Never forget the inestimable public relations value of *editorial* as opposed to *advertising*.

Accreditation of interviewee

It is very important that you make sure the media get your name and title right. If you don't tell them you're *not* the Chairman, you can't really blame them if they assume you are. You might well be 'king for a day', but your superiors won't be pleased.

You will remember that I stressed earlier the importance of finding out the name of your interviewer. Over-use of personal names quickly grates with the audience, but it is an extremely useful device when establishing the bond.

Correction of factual errors

If you remember how much journalists rely on their cuttings libraries, you will immediately appreciate how important it is to make sure that the final message that ends up on the screen or in print is the *right* one. Errors have a nasty habit of becoming perpetual if not checked swiftly. Remember, too, that media folk don't like to get it wrong either. Editors hate having to print corrections and journalists resent reprimands.

If you are half way through a live interview and you suddenly remember that the figure you quoted two minutes ago was incorrect, you must have the confidence to interrupt the flow of the current statement and set the record straight. It may feel awkward or cumbersome, but it has to be done.

If at the end of a recorded piece you realize you've made a mistake, again take the initiative and ask to re-record the relevant section. It is unlikely that your request will be refused.

Prior warning

There is no cardinal rule obliging a journalist to undergo the equivalent of metal detection screening before confronting you. But it is usually accepted that, if journalists do try to get through the security net, they run the risk of being politely asked the intention of their business and promised to be phoned back. Having prepared yourself as adequately as possible in the short time available, it is *imperative* that you do ring back.

Programme transcripts and copies

Unless we are dealing with an issue that involves national security, editors in all the three media disciplines will *rarely* agree to show an individual material prior to publication or transmission. As a practising broadcaster, I think this is fair. After all, you have had your chance to make your three points. Is it right that you should want to be programme maker as well?

What this limitation does highlight, yet again, is the importance of *preparation*. If you are confident, clear and in control, you're far more likely to come out well in an interview than if you are cowering, confused and out of control.

HOW TO MONITOR YOUR PERFORMANCE

Media people always seem to be in a hurry, rushing to get on to the next story. They don't appreciate requests from interviewees for audio or video cassettes, or copies of an article.

With regards to a radio or television programme, it is far simpler to find out the date and time of transmission, and record it yourself. Newspapers and magazines would obviously like you to buy the relevant issues on publication. It's worth remembering that, for a very modest sum, newspapers will send you print-outs of a particular article which can be used as an extremely effective publicity tool. The power of any favourable editorial copy is infinitely greater than advertisements.

If you are going to feature regularly in the press or appear on television or radio, there are two types of monitoring service which you'll find useful. **Tellex Monitors (47 Grays Inn Road, London WC1X 8PR, telephone: 071–405 7151)** is an organization with a head office in London and several regional ones, which monitor all national and local television and radio stations. They keep the tapes for a month, and on request can provide you with complete transcripts. A similar service is provided by **The Broadcast Monitoring Company (Register House, 4 Holford Yard, Cruikshanks Street, London WC1X 9HD, telephone: 071–833 1055)**. You do not necessarily have to subscribe to these services.

There are several agencies which, again by arrangement, will keep a newspaper cuttings file of either your company's press coverage or a related subject. Perhaps the most well known is **Romeike & Curtice (Hale House, Green Lane, London N13 5TP, telephone: 081–882 0155)**. Their office usually sends a batch of mounted cuttings out every month. As with Tellex Monitors and The Broadcast Monitoring Company, it's a valuable service, simply because it should winkle out the coverage you've missed.

Detailed list of questions

Even if they *were* willing to give you such detailed information, few reporters come armed with a *complete* list of questions. A good reporter will have mentally prepared a skeleton interview of about five questions, and will have researched sufficiently to follow you with intelligent supplementaries. And the unintelligent interviewer? Remember the rule – the question is merely a catalyst for your thoughts.

Veto on certain questions

Jeremy Paxman is a trenchant TV interviewer who expresses his views on this subject with a fiery eloquence. Asked to comment on what he does if a politician asks for a certain question not to be asked, he replied:

> Well, there may be all sorts of legitimate reasons for certain questions not being asked, legal reasons, questions of privacy, intrusion into private grief and so on. Those are the legitimate reasons for not asking a question, and you can accede such a request. But there are politicians who say, 'If you ask me that question, you will regret it', 'if you ask me that question, I will take it up with the Director General', 'if you ask me that question I will walk out'.
>
> Now clearly, it tends to concentrate the mind a bit when you are on in twenty seconds and a politician is saying that to you. My *personal* view is that, unless the question falls into that first category, you absolutely *have* to ask it. If you were going to ask it and you choose not to do so, then you betray the people whom you're supposed to be representing, on whose behalf you're putting the question. So you have to put it, you can't possibly agree to those attempts of blackmail or bullying.
> (*The Media Show*, Channel 4, 29 October 1989)

Running order

Your ability to insist on where you appear in the running order really depends on how badly a programme needs your presence. A government minister might well be able to dictate his terms. It's unlikely that, say, an industry spokesperson would. After all, if you're going to be troublesome, there are thousands more where you came from.

Remember

- Be prepared.
- Decide whether you want to take part.
- Research the programme or publication and its audience.
- Make a list of all your positive arguments and edit them to three.
- Address yourself to the negatives.
- Assert your rights.
- Practise, practise, practise.

4 What to expect in an interview

Despite the proliferation of radio, television and the printed word, most people have never been inside a radio of television studio or been interviewed by the press. It's hardly surprising, therefore, that the initial flurry of conceit in response to an invitation is quickly replaced by panic.

Not unlike an approaching dental appointment, the anticipation of anguish greatly outweighs the potential benefit. Like surgeries, television and radio studios are full of intimidating and unfamiliar equipment and, although its operators don't wear white coats, they have the same obvious advantages of being familiar and at ease with their environment. The combination of a specialist's assumed authority and the threatening recording equipment reduces the bravest patient's confidence. A studio and its staff can have the same effect on an inexperienced interviewee as a dentist can on a patient; the only difference is the extraction of truth rather than of teeth.

So long as you are rigorous in your preparation, and you know what to expect, you should have no difficulty in getting your message across, however hostile or lethargic the interviewer.

What to expect in a radio studio

 The most unflattering way to describe a person's looks is to talk about them having a great face for radio. And there is a grain of truth in the observation. Whilst radio is not exclusively staffed by the camera-shy, it does seem to attract individuals slightly less obsessed with ego than their TV counterparts.

But don't let the informality of radio folk and their shabby-chic studios lull you into a false sense of security. All journalists, of whichever discipline, want to prove a point, usually their own.

Of the three mediums discussed in this book, radio is the most intimate for both parties – participant and listener. It is also the least distracting. Not only does the broadcaster appear to be talking directly to a listener, but the listener is considerately allowed to get on with his shaving, tea-making and duvet-turning at the same time.

What it lacks, of course, is the colour and movement of television, and the benefits of newspaper photographs and layout techniques. Every picture, emotion and sensation has to be created aurally. Effective radio broadcasting is a refined skill, true exponents of which are few. What they all have in common is the ability to communicate on a *one-to-one* basis. It's one of the aims of this book to show *you* how to acquire this skill.

Radio and television don't need the oratorial tricks practised by the great orators of the early twentieth century. Indeed, excessive gesture on television often leaves you wide open to ridicule, and soaring voice levels on radio only serve to deafen your audience.

When you're appearing on either radio or television, imagine you are talking to *one person*. I've already mentioned an intelligent twelve-year-old. A broadcasting colleague of mine has a picture of a 'slightly deaf, middle-aged woman in Swindon'. It doesn't really matter what image you conjure, so long as it's a person you like and to whom you can relate. Adopting this communication technique should go a long way to conquering the terror of talking to millions.

The introduction of the 'advice phone-in' has taken radio communication to hitherto unimagined heights of intimacy. Anna Raeburn and Capital's Radio Doctor – Anna and the Doc – used to deal every week with a variety of live phone calls from London's troubled inhabitants. Such was the power of both broadcasters to appear to be dealing *directly* with each caller, that the appropriateness of some of the subjects discussed was sometimes called into question. How, you may wonder, was it possible for a man publicly to discuss his impotence 'on air'? Whatever his psychological motives, that caller exemplified the treatment of radio as a one-to-one medium.

Television and newspapers have numerous props with which to embellish their message. Apart from a library of sound effects, radio has none. Colour, emotion and passion rely essentially on the spoken word.

Churchill's broadcasts to the nation during the Second World War have already been cited as examples of effective communication. Here is another 'word picture', from the late Richard Dimbleby, who began his career in radio. The year was 1945 and he was reporting on his visit to the Nazi extermination camp Belsen:

> I passed through the barrier and found myself in the world of a nightmare. Dead bodies, some of them in decay, lay strewn about the road and along the rutted tracks. On either side of the road were brown wooden huts. There were faces at the windows, the bony emaciated faces of staring women too weak to come outside, propping themselves against the glass to see the daylight before they died – and they *were* dying – every hour, every minute.
>
> I saw a man wandering dazedly along the road, stagger and fall. Someone else looked down at him, took him by the heels and dragged him to the side of the road to join the other bodies lying unburied there. No one else took the slightest notice, they didn't even trouble to turn their heads.
>
> One woman, distraught to the point of madness, flung herself at a young British soldier who was on guard at the camp on the night it was reached by the 11th armoured division. She begged him to give her some milk for the tiny baby she held in her arms. She laid the mite on the ground, threw herself at the sentry's feet, and kissed his boots. And when, in distress, he asked her to get up, she put the baby in his arms and ran off crying that she would find milk for it, as there was no milk in her breast.

85

When the soldier opened the bundle of rags, to look at the child, he found it had been dead for days.

Unlike Richard Dimbleby, you may not have the luxury of time when composing your word pictures, but always remember to aim for the emotional rather than the statistical impact.

It's worth remembering that, in radio, your main contact will be either the programme producer or the News Editor. If time allows, it is best to write first, then phone, unless of course you have already established contact. However egalitarian the media may *appear* to be, like many institutions it relies heavily on the 'old boy network'. 'It is not *what* you know, but *who* you know.'

I said at the beginning of this book, the industry needs you just as much as you need it. Proof of this psychological table-turning is demonstrated by the media's 'OMG' factor.

'Oh, my God', or similar, *unprintable* appeals to the deity, occur daily – usually as a result of the breaking of a news story or a sudden unexpected collapse of part of a programme. People do occasionally fall sick, miss trains or forget. A last-minute cancellation is a producer's waking nightmare. A carefully balanced programme quickly falls apart if one of the guests, for whatever reason, can't appear. This is where *you*, the assiduous contact, have your moment of glory. No producer can afford 'dead' airtime. So, if the producer knows you're a good talker and can entertain the listeners, and you happen to have been speaking to him or her yesterday, then you could find yourself on radio. The producer's Bible is a contacts book, and it's your job to make sure you're in it.

Let's assume you're the branch manager of a local travel agent, and over the past few months you've been making a concerted effort to get to know your local radio station. You've taken part in its charity fund-raising events, displayed its publicity material in your shops and taken some spot advertising. You've also established a minor reputation with the station as being a good communicator.

A story breaks one morning of the collapse of a tour operator. The 'OMG' factor swings immediately into operation at the radio station. Who will come in, at very short notice, to talk about the situation? Because you've made *your* presence known, it's more than likely that, as far as travel matters are concerned, you'll be foremost in a producer's mind, and therefore it'll be *you* rather than your *competitor* who gets the opportunity to talk to present and future customers.

So what can you expect in a radio studio and on what type of programme might you find yourself?

There are essentially two types of voice studio: engineer-controlled and self-operated.

Engineer-controlled studio

This is the studio in which you are most likely to find yourself being interviewed.

The *engineer* sits behind a consul, usually facing the studio, but separated from you (in the voice booth) by a glass sound-proofed panel. The *producer* works with the engineer in the control room, deciding on the running order of stories, spooling in items already on tape and ushering guests in and out of the studio. He or she keeps in constant contact with the presenter either via the TV monitor, on which the instructions will be typed, or through the head-phones. The *presenter*, disc jockey or reporter (i.e. the person chairing the session) will usually sit at the head of the table in the studio.

You will be directed to your seat by the producer, who will probably have met you in reception. Producers' greetings are often warmer than their farewells. This apparent shift in affection mustn't be taken personally. Studios are very busy places and their personnel don't have time to indulge in ego boosting after the event. That doesn't mean, however, that they are averse to your boosting *their* egos. Just as an interviewer unerringly responds to pre-broadcast flattery, so a note to a producer after the show certainly won't go amiss.

ESTABLISHING A BOND

Once in the studio, it is very important to make sure that your seat is the right height and that, as far as possible, you can establish eye contact with the presenter. If time allows, and you're not walking into an 'on air' studio, greet your presenter and the other guests warmly.

It is appropriate, at this stage, to introduce you to the *fundamental* approach to an interviewer. Whether your interview is with someone from radio, television or the press, it is likely to be a highly charged, artificial encounter. Think about it. Two people who have never met are expected to talk to one another, usually under severe time constraints, as if it were the most natural thing in the world.

You have *one immediate priority*: to establish a *bond* with the interviewer. Management consultants claim that the first impression is made within ten seconds. In a radio or television studio, it is probably even less. If you fail to establish the bond, you can never hope to get your points across effectively.

VOICE LEVELS

As well as feeding any appropriate music, jingles or prerecorded items into the programme, it is the engineer's job to monitor all the levels of the individual speakers and to balance them before they are transmitted. Imagine how irritating it would be for the listener to have to adjust personally to the different pitch of each speaker. Once everyone is assembled, the presenter will ask for 'level' in order to give the engineer the opportunity to balance the voices.

It's industry norm, on both TV and radio, to ask as bland a question as possible to generate speech. A practice thought to have originated with the late Jack de Manio on the BBC Radio 4 *Today* programme, when the breakfasts used to be worthy of comment, you will probably be asked to recall your breakfast menu, to which the reply should on no account be 'nothing'. If you don't eat breakfast, make one up. Or, far more useful, use the time to exercise one of your fundamental rights by asking what the first question is going to be. Be sure, once you've given a voice level, that you stick to it. Engineers like an easy life, and the less attention they have to pay to those flickering needles the better.

Even former American Presidents are required to undergo the simple microphone test before a broadcast. And you would have thought that President Reagan would have known that a radio studio is as public a place 'off air' as it is 'on'. Apparently not. In preparing to record his weekly radio broadcast, Reagan was asked to perform the usual ritual of voice level. He obligingly responded, this time with joking extemporization:

> My fellow Americans, I am pleased to tell you we have signed legislation that would outlaw Russia forever. We begin bombing in five minutes.
> (*Daily Telegraph*, 14 August 1984)

Despite pleas from the White House that all voice-test remarks are 'off the record', the story broke in an American newspaper chain. He should have stuck to what he had for breakfast.

HEADPHONES

The presenter will probably wear headphones or 'cans', so called because of the sound quality produced by the early models, and may well have a TV monitor not visible to others. In most circumstances you won't need to wear headphones, the exceptions being the 'down the line' interview, and the phone-in (see pp.94, 95). The first experience of wearing headphones can be a little unnerving, as your voice will appear to be coming from your head rather than your mouth. To get a rough approximation of the sensation, put a finger in each ear and speak.

Just as we tend to speak more loudly when addressing foreigners, so people tend to react to the strange sensation of voice reverberation by raising the voice. Try, as far as you can, to maintain your normal level of speech. As each person's hearing sensitivity differs, you may well find that the sound of your voice in the 'cans' is far too loud. If this happens, tell the presenter, who will arrange for the engineer to turn the volume down. It's not that we deliberately set the headphone levels too high, simply that radio and television studios are very busy places and common courtesies can often get overlooked. Never be afraid to take the initiative and ask – it's in your interests to do so.

MICROPHONES

On your table or on the studio wall there might be a red and green light. A glowing *red* light indicates that a broadcast is in progress. Great care should be exercised when entering or exiting a studio, especially during a live transmission, to be as quiet as possible. An unguarded expletive when tripping over a studio chair could severely dent your credibility. Generally, a glowing *green* light indicates that communication is restricted to the control room and voice studio.

Each guest has his or her own microphone – sometimes an overwhelmingly large one. Try to resist the urge to engulf it, and be wary of using it as a loud-hailer. There is no need. However quiet your voice, the engineer will be able to adjust the microphone to accommodate you. Sometimes, if there aren't enough microphones to go round, you'll be asked to share. If this does happen, the engineer or the presenter will explain to you where to direct your voice.

When nervous, there is a tendency to wriggle, swivel and fidget. All these exercises should be strenuously avoided in a radio studio. Microphones are very sensitive, and what to you is occasional foot-tapping will sound to your listeners like a marching army. Rustling papers become autumn gales and clanking jewellery weighing anchors. And, although most microphones are multi-directional, if you swivel, the engineer will have to work extra hard to track you.

REFRESHMENT

All of us know what it's like to experience anxiety. Our palms sweat and our mouths dry. Naturally we attempt to salivate by feverishly licking our parched lips. Such is the cruelty of microphones that this innocent activity makes you sound as if you're the wearer of false teeth. To avoid the impression of dotage, always make sure you have either a glass of water or a cup of coffee in front of you.

Incidentally, tea is more refreshing than coffee as the latter tends to dehydrate. I doubt that it was due to media training, more to his particular life-style, but I remember watching Terence Stamp produce his own flask of tea before we began the interview. As Barry Norman would say, 'And why not?' *On no account should you accept alcohol.*

Smoking is not usually prohibited in a radio studio, but it is tactful, if you *really* feel you can't get by without a cigarette, to check with the presenter before lighting up.

THE INTERVIEW

During the interview, your *sole* concentration should be on the presenter, so long as you're the only person involved in the interview. Engineers aren't paid to pass editorial judgement, and the producer is concerned with the entire programme's output, not just your contribution.

Don't be alarmed if the presenter appears, now and again, not to be concentrating on what you're saying. It could be that you've failed to hold his or her interest, but it's far more likely that the presenter is taking instructions about the next item, or making adjustments to the line of questioning. Whatever the situation, unless directed otherwise, *carry on.*

Most inexperienced interviewees need a security blanket of some kind, usually in the form of an *aide-mémoire.* The most effective reminder is the simple index card, on which are written your three main points (highlighted) and a couple of examples. On the blank reverse side, make a note of the presenter's name and other studio guests. Unless you are to take part in a phone-in, there is no point in bringing sheaves of notes. You won't have time to look at them and, even if you try to, you won't be able to find your place and will lose ground in the eye-contact stakes.

It is only fair to warn you that, on some very fast-moving current affairs programmes, there won't be time to take any level, let alone to ask about the first question. Some presenters, too, will appear to be deeply preoccupied until a few seconds before going on air, simply because they don't want to engage in any kind of rehearsal that might jeopardize the interview. If you do find yourself in this uncomfortable situation, remember your three points, make sure you have water, take a deep breath and *listen extremely carefully* to the presenter's introduction, which will inevitably give you a clue to the tone of the forthcoming interview. It may even contain an error, the polite correction of which at the outset of the interview will earn you many listeners' points, and set you firmly in control.

It is sometimes possible to have an engineer record your item as it's transmitted. Bring a blank cassette with you as an incentive. I don't recommend setting up your own mini-mobile recording unit on the studio table. It will make the presenter suspicious and suspicion leads quickly to hostility.

The golden rule in radio or television is to ignore everyone except your interviewer, never lose sight of your audience, and try, at all times, to be *confident, clear* and *in control.*

Self-operated studio

Radio has always been the impoverished sister to television, and old inferiorities die hare. This is perhaps why many local radio stations cut their staffing and building costs by having their 'jocks' or presenters do the engineer's job as well as their own. They will not only conduct the interviews, but operate the desk, fire the cartridges for the commercials and jingles, and spin in the discs and tapes.

The atmosphere, although undeniably intimate, is often very cramped and distracting. Despite the obvious discomfort and distractions, the principles are exactly the same as in an engineer-controlled studio. You focus on your microphone and the interviewer and ignore everyone else.

Types of radio interview

Live

The obvious advantage of the live interview is you're not at the mercy of an editor. So long as you're well prepared, live performances are often sharper than pre-recorded ones.

Unfortunately, you're seldom afforded the luxury of time, either to familiarize yourself with the studio or to explain complicated points.

Recorded

Perhaps unknown to the listener, much of the output on BBC Radio, which includes the World Service, is pre-recorded. Location interviews, unless serviced by a radio car, will be recorded by a reporter on a simple tape machine, brought back to the studios and edited in readiness for transmission. The exceptions tend to be news broadcasts and daily current affairs and magazine programmes, although even those will contain an element of pre-recorded material. Because independent radio tends to work within very tight commercial margins, a great deal of *speech* output will be live.

There are advantages and disadvantages to the pre-recorded interview. On the positive side, a pre-recorded interview tends to be a little more relaxed than a live one. Everyone is secure in the knowledge that, if a mistake is made, it can always be corrected – which, indeed, it *must* be. There is also more time for the parties involved to get to know one another and to ask for the favour of a re-run if unhappy with the first take. Radio editing might be lethally precise (always a concern for an interviewee), but it is extremely quick and inexpensive to execute. Unless really pushed for time, no producer will refuse you the opportunity to re-record a section of the interview. Indeed sometimes, if the first take was too long and would have required extensive editing, they would welcome a re-record.

But there *are* pitfalls. A recorded interview can lull interviewees into a false sense of security, making them abandon their principles of *confidence, clarity and control*. The interviewee is also at the mercy of the razor blade. Much to people's surprise, magnetic tape is still edited in this quaintly old-fashioned way. On my first day as a junior reporter, consigned to the 'graveyard' shift and charged with phoning all the metropolitan police stations to learn of any overnight murders, muggings or fires, I was handed a box of blades. I remember wondering whether slashing one's wrists was commonplace in a radio news room.

Down the line

There are two kinds of interview where eye contact will be of no help: the 'down the line' and the telephone. In both cases you are talking to someone without the advantage of seeing them. For some, the anonymity does wonders for their lucidity, but for most, lack of visual contact reduces warmth in the voice and introduces unnatural stiffness.

'Down the line' is the technical term for the method by which locations can speak to one another via what is essentially a telephone line of superior quality. Such is the quality of the line that a listener, unless so informed, wouldn't know that the speakers could be hundreds of miles apart. The best way to overcome the absence of eye contact is to find an eye point in your studio, *imagine* a person directly in your eye line, and then talk to that imaginary figure rather than to a disembodied voice coming through your headphone. One indisputable advantage of a radio down the line or telephone interview is that no one can see you cribbing from your notes or grimacing at the studio engineer.

Telephone

In my early days as a radio reporter, as well as the razor blades we were issued with what looked like miniature bull-dog clips (affectionately known as crocodile clips) attached to two fine plastic-coated pieces of wire. By unscrewing the mouthpiece of a public telephone and attaching the clips to certain sensitive parts of its innards, it was possible to play a recorded interview direct to the studio. I still doubt the legality of the procedure and it's probably not practised today, but it certainly made imaginative use of the telephone. Your telephone interview will be much more straightforward – no clips, no wires.

The principles of conducting a telephone interview are exactly the same as those for a down the line, except that, as the quality of the reception will be less, it is very important that you speak clearly and a little more slowly. We've all heard a frustrated DJ beg his caller to turn his radio off. Remember to do so before you do your interview. If you don't, you'll create what is known as 'feedback' – an ear-piercing howling sound which, apart from hurting your eardrums, completely obliterates your message.

The great advantage of the telephone interview is that it is almost guaranteed to take place in your own familiar environment. Take the trouble to make sure that the interview goes as smoothly as possible. If you're in your office, make sure you're not interrupted. If you're at home, pay the kids to take the dog out.

Phone-in

Phone-ins are popular with both radio stations and their listeners. The radio stations like them because they are cheap to produce, and listeners seem to get vicarious pleasure out of hearing like-minded souls struggle to express their prejudices, opinions and innermost secrets.

The great advantage for *you* is the amount of airtime you'll be allotted. Anyone agreeing to take part in a phone-in can be assured of at least a 5–10 minute establishing interview, followed by 20 to 30 minutes of listeners' calls. Imagine how many opportunities that gives you to mention your organization or product. Overplugging will be discussed in Chapter 5.

Just because you're going to be talking to so-called 'ordinary' people, don't be lulled into thinking that your performance can be less polished than if you were talking to a professional broadcaster. If anything, it must be *more* so. Your research must be thorough, your knowledge wide and your patience endless. As with a down the line interview, you must try and visualize someone at the other end of the phone. Make a note of the caller's name and use it as and when appropriate. Although using a presenter's name must be approached with caution – over-use sounds insincere – this is rarely the case when talking to a caller.

Phone-in guests have to act a little like doctors. They must diagnose the symptoms from an initial description, ascertain the illness by further questioning, and offer some kind of treatment at the end. Never let the listener feel he or she is going away empty-handed.

Most inexperienced phone-in guests are anxious that they won't be able to control a caller. In the unlikely event that you find yourself embroiled in unproductive argument or, worse, receiving abuse, the presenter will invariably step in and bring the call to an abrupt close, cut the caller off or, in extreme circumstances, press the profanity button, which will fill in the ten-second broadcast delay with a station jingle, during which time the offending caller can be dismissed.

Radio car

The radio car comes in various guises, but is generally a large van or truck (Range Rovers are a popular choice), which is equipped to act as a mobile extension of a radio station and can be used for two purposes.

LIVE COVERAGE OF A NEWS STORY

If the radio car is called out on a news story, the news desk will use their outside broadcast engineers to operate the equipment. They will drive to the site where the interview is to take place, having been allocated a special radio frequency known as a 'programme quality radio link'. The interview will be conducted either in the radio car (only marginally less comfortable than the studio itself) or perhaps outside it. As with the 'down the line', you will be asked to wear headphones and you will not be able to see your interviewer. The interview and sound effects will be picked up by a receiver in the locality and relayed back to the radio station.

A talk-back system is used as a line of communication between the radio car and the master control room at the radio station. The engineers will also probably be listening to a portable radio to make sure that they time the insert correctly. If you do find yourself being interviewed in the radio car, make sure that someone tells you when you are chatting informally and when you're actually on air. Only recently the former chancellor Nigel Lawson had to be gently reminded that, unbeknownst to him, his thoughts were being shared by the *entire* Radio 4 *Today* audience.

THE OUTSIDE BROADCAST

Occasionally an entire afternoon's broadcasting will take place from the radio car, which will act as a portable studio. In this case you *will* see your interviewer.

An engineer will have surveyed the site in advance to determine the quality of the signal. If the signal isn't sufficiently strong, the engineer will book land-lines. None of these technical problems, of course, are any concern of yours. Remember, your focus is on your interviewer. Do, however nervous you may be feeling, exercise *patience*. Outside broadcasts are fraught with engineering problems, and agitated interviewees will only worsen the situation.

Syndicated

Syndicated radio is a good idea if you want to get your message across to local radio listeners around the country without having to visit the stations, which can be time consuming and costly. There are several companies who specialize in this type of radio production.

Producing a tape which is sent to around 35 local, mostly independent, radio stations will cost somewhere in the region of £650. Although the radio stations are under no obligation to play the tape, an average pick-up is about fourteen stations.

Apart from saving time and money, the other advantage of recording an interview for syndication is the degree of editorial control you can exert. You will be able to discuss the content and line of questioning with a producer, have time for a pre-on-air conversation with your interviewer and, if you're not happy with the first take, have another go.

As regards the number of company mentions during the interview, the unwritten rules of syndicated editorial are that you will be allowed one mention of your company/product in the introduction to the tape, one in the main body, and one in the presenter's back-announcement to the piece.

It's very important, if your interview is to have any chance of being picked up by the radio stations, that you have a strong 'angle'. For example, your company may be producing a schools' pack, for use in teaching as part of the new National Curriculum, or you may be sponsoring an exhibition of safety in the home. Local radio is interested in *general issues*, not *product promotions*.

It's also important, wherever possible to regionalize the interview. People living in Cornwall are seldom interested in the lives of those in Northumberland. If, for instance, your interview is talking about the regional differences in attitudes towards drinking, then make sure that you personalize, as far as you are able, the key geographical regions.

Unless you've got a fifteen-minute 'exclusive' with the Prince of Wales, the interviews you send shouldn't, after editing, be longer than five minutes. This may not look very long on paper, but it's *double* what you'd get on the *Today* programme.

BBC SYNDICATED RADIO

Under the auspices of **Programme Services (Broadcasting House, Great Portland Street, London W1A 1AA, telephone: 071–580 4468)**, the BBC also pre-record interviews for syndication to the BBC local radio network. They use their extensive 'down the line' facilities to distribute the pieces, which are usually about six minutes long. The stations are only charged for the longer half-hour documentary programmes which are copied on to tape, boxed and posted to the stations.

Obviously, BBC local radio cannot be seen to endorse a company or product but, if you can convince them that you have a strong story (e.g. the results of a survey, the publication of a book, etc.), then they might well record an interview. The BBC don't charge for this facility.

Remember on radio

- Make sure you know the style of the programme and its presenter's name.
- Arrive at a radio studio about twenty minutes before the broadcast. On *no* account be late.
- Never dress down for radio.
- Avoid clanking jewellery and digital watches.
- Make sure bleepers are switched off and that you never bring a portable phone into the studio.
- Always have a small card index bearing your three main points, and a pencil with you.
- Try not to smoke.
- Never accept alcohol, but always make sure you have some kind of liquid refreshment – preferably water.
- Don't engulf the microphone.
- Don't swing on your chair.
- A red light indicates 'on air' – anything you say or do could be heard by millions.
- Never assume that an interview is over until you are told that it is.
- Make sure you maintain eye-contact throughout the interview.
- Remember to smile. In radio especially, when you smile your voice smiles with you.
- Nothing is off the record. If you don't want anyone to know about it, don't say it.

What to expect in a television studio

Television must battle to win the viewer's attention against formidable odds. Watching television used to be an occasion, during which time people would devote their *whole* attention to a programme. People have now become so blasé about the medium that only the addictive 'soaps' can claim such concentration. There are also many distractions in a home – telephone, children, pets, doorbells, all competing for attention. Television, by offering so much choice, is almost its own worst enemy. As our boredom thresholds diminish, so our tendency to channel-hop increases. A television viewer is a far harsher critic than his or her professional counterpart, and won't wait to see if the programme improves before moving on.

Television, if you don't know how to conduct yourself, can also appear to do radical things to your body and personality. What to friends is an endearing facial twitch can make you look half-witted on the screen. It also exaggerates the display of emotions. If you're feeling anxious, you'll look terrified. If you have a tendency to fidget, you'll look as if you have ants in your pants. The irony of television is that, whilst no one doubts its power unless you know how to harness it, you could do yourself more harm than good by appearing on it.

If the odds are so heavily stacked against you, is there really point in a rank amateur trying to exploit the medium?

There is and you must.

Television is watched by *millions*, 24 hours a day. With the seemingly endless growth in outlets (satellite, cable, a fifth channel and so on), the search for material is going to get more and more intense, which means your chances of getting yourself on television are going to increase proportionally. They need you as much as you need them.

The proliferation of business programmes on television reflects the nation's growing interest in financial affairs, which again increases your opportunity to get the message across.

And, perhaps most important of all, your company probably couldn't afford to buy television advertising time, but it could, if it fielded the right person and got its story right, get *free* television exposure.

The most you can hope to register with a television audience is an *impression*, but that is no bad thing. If a viewer remembers you for your nice smile, or sincerity, you've succeeded in using television to your advantage.

Where will it all begin?

Because the economics of radio dictate a small workforce, the position of *researcher* doesn't exist in that medium. But in the more opulent world of television he or she is the person you are most likely to encounter before you get anywhere near the studio. Generally, researchers will be fairly junior, and it will be their job to check out your story and assess your ability to deliver the goods. The first approach will usually be made by phone, followed by a meeting in your office, the purpose of which will be to continue the research and conduct a reconnoitre ('recce') for the film crew if your interview is to be filmed on location. If the story is for a news programme, the researcher will often dispense with the preliminary visit and simply arrive with the film crew and reporter ready to record the interview.

Television has a bewildering number of personnel. Unless you want to get embroiled in the hierarchy, the only two people with whom you really need to concern yourself are the researcher and the reporter or the interviewer. If you'd feel more confident armed with a who's who in a television studio, you should know that the *producer* is in charge of the programme's housekeeping, the *director* decides what the viewer will see, and an *editor* will be in overall charge. The *specialist correspondent* is equivalent to a reporter, as is a *presenter*.

The studio

To the inexperienced eye, a television studio is a place designed to look after everyone except you. They all seem to be in a frenzy and speaking in a foreign language. Snaking black cables, glinting camera lenses and crazily positioned arc lights all add to the victim's general terror.

The golden rule in a television studio before you go 'on air' is to do as you're told and focus your attention *solely* on your interviewer. Whatever you do, don't try and engage in humorous banter with camera operators. Interviews with no illustrative relief, 'talking head' interviews as they're derisively known in television, are anathema to camera operators, who'd

101

much rather be on the streets of Belfast than stuck with the limited responsibility of offering the director the alternative of a close-up or a very close-up of yours truly.

The most distracting person in the studio is the *floor manager*. The floor manager's job is to relay messages from the director, who sits literally on high, in a glass box (the gallery) overlooking the studio, to the reporter or presenter. Prior to transmission the floor manager can, of course, talk to everyone. But as soon as the red light goes on, he or she must resort to sign language. The combination of a crouched position below the camera lenses and strange gesticulations make the floor manager hard to ignore. I defy anyone to disregard someone appearing to give you a V-sign or cut you off in your prime by drawing their hand sharply across their neck. These symbols are not a reflection on your performance, but are simply silent time signals to the reporter. The apparent insult of the two-finger gesture will inform an interviewer that there are two minutes left to talk, and the severing action across the throat indicates that the interview must be brought to an end *immediately*.

Studio interviewers will be asked to wear a small ear-piece, through which they will receive constant verbal instructions from the director. Most broadcasters, myself included, resent ear-pieces but accept them as a necessary link between the studio and the control box. It's worth remembering, when your interviewer's eyes seem to have gone to another land, that he or she is probably taking instructions about the next item.

The only time conflict arises between the director and/or producer and the interviewer and the ear-piece is when the producer, with no prior warning, decides that the interview should be going in a direction totally contrary to the interviewer's planned route. Interviewers can't answer back and mustn't show any displeasure. They must try somehow to accommodate the producer *and* keep up a conversation. And you thought *your* role was difficult.

Television technicians are highly paid and guard their jobs jealously. That is why, when a sound engineer comes to pin a microphone to your tie or lapel, you don't attempt to help. If you do, you could cause a union walk-out. Microphones used in television studios are known as 'neck mics' because they are normally clipped fairly close to your neck. They are small and unobtrusive, but just as sensitive as those used in a radio studio. So *don't* wear the family jewels if they're likely to strike the microphone.

Despite such restrictions, it is *very* important that you don't lose sight of some of the basic rights talked about in Chapter 3. If there isn't a glass of water, ask for one. If the chair seems about to collapse, make sure you have one that won't. Studio guests often complain about the design of studio chairs or sofas. The former are often the wrong height and swivel; the latter should be banned. If something *is* blocking your direct eye-line with your interviewer, tell him or her. Interviewers don't *deliberately* set out physically to trip you up. Mentally maybe, but not physically.

Rehearsal

If you find yourself involved in a technically complicated television programme, you may well be asked to sit through a rehearsal, during which lighting provision and camera shots are established.

This can be an extremely boring experience. It's often tempting, in order to relieve the monotony, to start discussing some of the points you are intending to make during the interview. Don't. Talk about the weather, your children, hobbies – anything but the real reasons why you're in the studio.

Green room

Television, unlike radio, has a green room, a description borrowed from the theatre, which is where you are likely to be taken before going into the studio. Another name is the 'hospitality suite' (or, as Terry Wogan calls it, 'hostility suite'). This room can be used to your advantage or your detriment.

If you have your wits about you, you'll quickly find out the identity of everyone else in the room, you'll talk to the researcher or producer to try and find out a little more about the structure of the interview, and you'll generally convey an aura of confidence and co-operation. Very occasionally, you might meet your interviewer. I make a point of *not* meeting my interviewees because I want to preserve all my energies for the interview itself. If you are fortunate enough to have a few minutes with the interviewer beforehand, use the time wisely. Run over the general parameters again, find out how the interview will start, and bring to his or her attention any new information. But be wary, in your eagerness to please, of saying too much.

If you allow your nerves to dominate, you'll greedily accept the free gin and tonics, exude a sense of panic, be totally unable to focus on yourself, let alone anyone else, and probably divulge far too much information.

Release form

If you agree to be interviewed on television or radio, you could be asked to sign a Form of Release, probably before the interview takes place, but sometimes afterwards.

Although the wording of the form varies from company to company, by signing the document you are effectively handing over the rights of the interview to the company, who retain the right to edit and broadcast it. The form also often serves as a financial contract.

In some politically sensitive situations, an interviewee can persuade a programme producer to allow him to preview the programme before he signs the form.

Alcohol

A serious design fault as far as man and the media is concerned is what happens to him when he drinks alcohol. Relaxation of the nervous system is just what we *don't* want in television. The programme makers do: they'd love to have you with your guard down, which is why they ply you with alcohol in the green room. And it is very tempting. You're feeling anxious

104

and you know from experience that a couple of drinks always relax you.

In a state of heightened nervous tension, alcohol will play havoc with your performance. Not only will the combination of the heat from the studio lights and your expanded capillaries make you appear to be suffering from severe sunburn, but the alcohol in your blood stream will affect your brain and con it into believing that you are equipped with the incisiveness of Robin Day, the clarity of Michael Heseltine or the persuasiveness of Margaret Thatcher. What happens in reality is that you sweat, your tongue swells, you lose concentration and you're lucky if you can get across *one*, let alone all *three* of your points.

I still blush when I remember how an innocent tipple nearly cost me my job. The one chore of presenting a live evening arts show was how to fill in the time between the end of an official working day and the broadcast. Whereas Fleet Street had little to offer in food venues, it abounded with drinking haunts to which I would go most evenings, for the company rather than the alcohol. But one fateful night caution forsook me.

My star guests were to be the incomparable duo Morecambe and Wise – quite a coup for a local radio station. Although looking forward to the interview, I was nervous. Comedians are difficult people with whom to have a meaningful conversation, and even more so if you are a little in awe of them. To quell the knocking knees and churning stomach, I broke my cardinal rule and allowed myself to be persuaded into drinking a glass of wine – which quickly became two and, although I can't swear to it, perhaps a third.

It was a distinctly flushed, wobbly presenter who found her way back to the studio that evening. Too late to back out, I prayed for the miracle cure of black coffee and a lot of commercial breaks. Neither helped. The interview was a disaster. I was told by a none-too-pleased editor the next morning that I had appeared to try to match wit for wit with the mighty duo and that my news reading was barely intelligible. I deserved to be fired and was lucky not to be. I have certainly *never* taken a drink before an interview since.

105

The interview

Your visit to the green room could last for anything from ten minutes to half an hour, or even longer if the programme is to be recorded. When the time is right, you will be collected by a member of the programme team, probably a researcher, and either taken into make-up or shown to your place in the studio from where you'll be made up. Television make-up is far more subtle than it used to be, but it's still advisable for men to remove it before leaving the building. Once made up, you will probably be fixed with a microphone, levels will be taken, you'll meet your interviewer and, before you know what's happened, it will all be over.

It is important to remind you again that the one person on whom you focus *all* your attention is the interviewer. *Never* try to find your camera. Terry Wogan can because he's been in the business a long time. It will simply make *you* look foolish. The two exceptions to looking at the interviewer and never looking directly into the camera occur during a group discussion, when you obviously look at the person you're addressing, and when you've been instructed by the director to look into a camera. For instance, if you're demonstrating a piece of equipment, a close-up of the product will be dedicated to one particular camera, to which you will be asked to point at the appropriate time.

Most studios are equipped with four cameras. One will offer a general shot of the set, known as the 'wide shot', another will be trained on the presenter, another on you, and the final one will be used for illustrative material. Whilst it is true that the glowing red light just above the camera indicates that this is the one whose image is being beamed into our homes, resist the temptation to follow it.

If you do have to speak directly to a camera, as you will if you do a 'down-the-line' television interview, look directly into the centre of the lens. Looking above or below it somehow makes you look shifty.

Can you bring a friend with you into the studio? It's perfectly natural to want a bit of moral support before an interview. Indeed, it's a good idea to see if someone *can* come with you, if only to sort out any administrative problems. He or she might be able to accompany you to the green room, but it's very unlikely you'll be allowed to walk hand in hand into the studio.

Thoughtful producers, after the interview, will invite you back to the green room, where you can wind down and relax. But not too much – you're still on duty, and people are taking a note of what you're saying.

Types of television interview

Live

Live television tends to be the exception rather than the rule, which perhaps explains why, when it is live, programme-makers go to great lengths to remind the viewer of the novelty by festooning the studio with clocks and giving constant verbal time checks.

Live chat shows will still conduct lighting and camera rehearsals, in which you could be involved. But on daily current affairs programmes you will have as little 'warm-up' time as on live radio.

Recorded

Just as with radio, there are advantages and disadvantages to the recorded television interview. The atmosphere is certainly less tense and people appear to have a little more time. The time of recording is usually more hospitable, which will give you the opportunity for even more preparation.

On the other hand, you will have no control over which parts of your contribution they'll include, or, necessarily, who else might appear in the programme, or at which point during the proceedings you'll be introduced. By all means try asking – not in an accusatory fashion, but simply as a seeker of information. As I have been at pains to point out throughout this book, media folk like to be treated as human beings. Treat them well and, on the whole, they will respond favourably.

107

If you make a factual mistake during a recorded interview, you *must* correct it. Don't be intimidated by mutterings of overtime costs. This is *your* moment, and although they won't admit it, they don't want to get it wrong either. As VTR (video) editing is expensive, you shouldn't be surprised if the whole interview is re-done. This should work to your advantage but won't if you try and remember what you said the first time. However many 'takes' there are, treat each one as a completely *new* interview; that way you will avoid tripping yourself up.

Down the line

The art of talking convincingly to an inanimate object is very skilled indeed. Most people find it difficult and come across as either slow-witted or deaf. If you master it, it's an expedient way of getting your message across if you're not able to be there in person.

You will be directed to a very small studio, sat in front of a single camera and asked to put in the ear-piece. Before you know what's happened, you're 'on air'. To help you look half-way human:

- Avoid looking at the TV monitor, which will probably show you the studio to which you are linked.
- Look directly into the middle of the camera lens.
- Make sure your ear-piece fits.
- Try to move your head from time to time, and don't be afraid of gesture.

I've noticed a growing tendency in people (especially politicians) doing down-the-line interviews to suddenly appear to lose audio contact with the interviewer at the moment the questions get tough. It's not a ploy I would recommend an inexperienced interviewee adopting.

Remember on television

- Make sure you know the style of the programme and its presenter's name.
- Television complexes often have more than one studio. Make sure you know exactly which one to go to. If a car isn't picking you up, try and get a friend to drive you, and plan the route beforehand.
- Arrive about fifteen minutes before you've been asked.
- If the receptionist appears to know nothing about you, produce the relevant documents and *insist* that the programme producer is informed.
- Never drink alcohol in the green room, but make sure you have some liquid in the studio.
- Allow yourself to be made up.
- Try and ignore everything going on around you except your interviewer.
- Never try to find the 'on air' camera, and never look directly into the camera lens unless so instructed.
- Allow the technicians to do their jobs without interference.
- Don't smoke.
- Don't bring sheaves of notes into the studio.
- Try and find out when a recorded programme will be transmitted, so you can arrange for it to be recorded. Television studios and radio stations are not very willing to make copies for you.
- After an interview, make a note of the relevant people involved. It is much easier to go to a named contact with your next story. A note of thanks to the programme is always appreciated.
- Nothing is off the record.
- Always correct a mistake (either live or recorded).

What to expect in a location interview

In theory, a taped conversation conducted on home territory shouldn't cause you as much anxiety as a studio one. And, indeed, if you're aware of some of the technicalities involved, it won't.

But before you agree to a local or national television or radio crew recording on your premises, remember to assert some of your basic rights.:

- For which particular programme are you being interviewed?
- What's the angle of the story?
- Who else will they be talking to?
- Suggest an appropriate place to film: for example, in your office, on the factory floor, or on the top of the building.

As the first three points have already been dealt with at length in Chapter 3, only the fourth need concern us here.

Location crews are *always* in a hurry and although, unlike their studio counterparts, they do have a legitimate excuse to submit travel expenses, they still tend to be as cynical and world-weary as studio crews. For this reason, unless they're accompanied by a Richard Attenborough, they'll simply point the camera at you and shoot. ENG (electronic news gathering) crews consist of a camera operator, a sound man or woman, who often doubles up as a lighting engineer, and a reporter. If the story is to be part of a documentary, the director or the producer might also attend, but on the whole news stories will field a skeleton team.

As ITN reporter Joan Thirkettle remarks, they move *fast*:

If you're on a typical news story where there is no hanging around, the actual picture you need is nearby and everybody is ready, you would probably be filming for about one hour, and that would include the interview which would be five to ten minutes. If you're really up against it, it could be done in 20 minutes. That footage, which would include the interviewee's piece of about 20 to 30 seconds, depending on the strength of his delivery, would be edited to a story package of a maximum two and a half minutes, but more often about one minute thirty.

There are exceptions to the 30 second 'sound bite'. During the coverage of the Eniskillen bomb on 11 November 1987, Gordon Wilson lost his daughter Marie, who was a nurse. He felt he wanted to tell the world, via the media, what an extraordinarily special person his daughter was. There was no question of seeking revenge – in his view, that was a negative emotion. That interview was run at length because it was so powerful. Here was a man expressing his innermost feelings in a profoundly moving way.

Choosing the right location

As news reporters are as often as not on the run, they may not pay as much attention to choosing the best place to record the interview as you would like. Giving suggestions to a television crew can be a sensitive business. So always be tactful.

Supposing you're being quizzed on your environmental record as a local factory. To be standing in front of the factory chimney as it belches smoke will discredit the strongest of statement. Far better than you're seen on the football field of the company sports club.

Perhaps the safest location is your office. You'll feel much more comfortable in a familiar environment and you might even be able to position your company logo strategically behind you so that it will have an unobtrusive presence during the interview.

However much the crew seem to be pressed for time, never forget to exert some of your rights before the camera starts to record:

● What are the broad parameters of the interview?
● How long will the interview run?
● What's the first question?

Joan Thirkettle, speaking here for many of her colleagues

whose reporting work is done almost *entirely* on location, has her own 'rules of the game':

> If someone asks me what the questions are going to be before we record, I invariably tell them that the interview will be very straightforward, and I will ask them about what is happening and what the outcome will be.
>
> I will have prepared the interview in my head beforehand – I never work from a crib sheet – and I will ask supplementary questions as and when they arise.
>
> If the interviewee makes a mistake he should say so. It's in everyone's interests to get it right. If an interviewee asks to see the edited version of a story before it is broadcast, the answer is, almost without an exception, 'No'.

We've already touched on the dangers of responding to reporters' questions with a curt 'no comment'. Joan Thirkettle believes that this can be detrimental as it indicates that the interviewee is trying to hide something. There are sometimes legitimate reasons for a 'no comment' reply – when a situation is *sub judice* for example – in which case the interviewee should always say so.

The interview

For simplicity's sake, let's assume that you are to be interviewed in your office. Make sure that you're *not interrupted*. Telephones, messengers and unruly fax machines should all be silenced. Please don't spring clean your premises, as this will make you look stiff and unnatural in your surroundings. Do make sure, however, that evidence of last night's revelries have been disposed of, and that your wall calendar tells the right date. All very minor details, but just the kind of thing an unkind viewer will alight upon. Result – evaporation of concentration on you and the transference to an inanimate object.

Unlike a studio crew, which usually boasts three or four cameras, a location crew will, unless it's an outside broadcast unit, be equipped with only one. This severely limits the visual opportunities. The restrictions are usually overcome by the inclusion of what are known as 'noddies'.

During the interview, the camera will be focused on you. In order to establish the presence of the reporter, and provide essential edit points, the reporter will be filmed subsequently asking the questions again. The reporter will also be asked to tilt the head, nod, smile, adopt an expression of deep interest and so on. To your embarrassment, you might also be asked to join in this pantomime by pretending to be listening intensely to a question or by seeming to be involved in an animated discussion. Whilst you may feel rather foolish, the important thing to remember is that the exercise is being done not to *trick* you, but simply to broaden the visual scope of the interview.

As well as the interview, the story may well include 'establishing' material. This is another opportunity for you to try and exert some influence. The reporter may well not know that, at the rear of your factory site, you have a brand new depot. By taking the initiative and showing her, you could take control of the story, and change her approach.

Once the filming is over, do offer the crew some hospitality. Remember to take no alcohol yourself. This is your chance to turn the tables. It's often during an informal debriefing that you learn much more about the programme and its contents. Do ask when the item will be transmitted, and make sure someone records it for you.

There are *rare* occasions when you'll be filmed at a location other than home territory. Exactly the same rules apply. Remember, though, to find out beforehand where you're going, and with whom you might be speaking.

I've no doubt that Michael Foot, then leader of the Labour Party, wished he had taken that precaution during the Mitcham and Morden by-election in the summer of 1982. Ed Boyle was working for Thames Television at the time:

We were parked outside the Labour Party headquarters in Mitcham to await the arrival of Michael Foot. The Rover, with official driver and Mr Foot's minder, duly arrived and I had a few words with the leader, who subsequently made to leave for the headquarters. We kept our cameras rolling to get shots of him and his Labour Party colleagues. To our surprise, he didn't

113

walk into the HQ, which was a humble suburban dwelling, but into a tyre replacement garage next door. And so our cameras were able to follow him being redirected by the staff. And those, of course, were the pictures that appeared. However eloquent his words may have been, the viewer was left with the image of the then leader of the Labour Party not being able to find his local party headquarters.

Remember on location

- Make sure there are no interruptions.
- Find the most suitable location for the interview.
- Be accommodating.

What to expect in a press interview

A print journalist, novelist Rebecca West, described journalism as 'an ability to meet the challenge of filling the space'. Whilst many of the principles of successful interviews apply as much to the printed word as they do to radio or television, the key difference is the amount of time you're likely to spend with a press journalist.

Face to face

As we have seen, a radio or television interview can be as little as 60 seconds long and seldom lasts more than fifteen minutes (unless you're a leading politician who agrees to an hour with Brian Walden). One-to-one newspaper journalist interviews are seldom *shorter* than half an hour. For the well prepared, a journalist's interview presents 30 minutes of opportunity. For those who haven't troubled to do their homework, it's a potential mine-field.

114

A constant complaint against the printed media is its apparent disregard for fact and its habitual misquoting. I don't deny that some newspapers *do* invent stories. Some people, too, are quoted out of context. But, to use a legal concept, this is not always with deliberate intent to pervert the truth.

Most day-to-day print reporters will have several stories going at one time. They are under constant pressure from their editors to meet deadlines. The combination of your muddled thinking and their time constraints can all too easily lead to a rushed summation of your statements, rather than accurate quotes.

The rules for dealing with journalists are as follows:

- Always appear friendly and helpful, especially during the initial enquiry to arrange a meeting. If possible, arrange for the interview to be on your territory and make sure you've familiarized yourself with the publication and, if possible, the journalist's work. Find out if there's a deadline.

- Anticipate the questions. This is not difficult. The journalist will be asking the same type of questions as his or her television or radio counterpart: who, what, why, where, when and how. Treat the journalist purely as a conduit for your opinions. Don't be surprised if journalists come with their own preconceptions and angles to the story. If they didn't, neither of you would get anywhere. Don't be afraid to ask if there's an angle to the story. Once you know, you can then artfully steer the journalist towards your own.

- Prepare your three main points and make sure you bring them in during the interview. As you are likely to cover much more ground with a print journalist, it's important to take control at the *end* of the interview to re-establish the three points: 'Is there anything else you need from me? From my point of view, the three most important areas we've covered are ...'

- The spiral notebook seems to have gone very much out of fashion these days, replaced by the cassette recorder (both could be used as legal documents in a court of law). If a

115

journalist produces one before the interview, don't be afraid to produce your own. On *no* account try to record the interview surreptitiously. Journalists will smell a rat a mile away and, if they suspect you of underhand play, their resentment will probably be reflected in the piece.

- Just as with radio and television, treat everything after the initial greeting as on the record.

- Be wary, too, of the old journalist's trick of presenting you with a long convoluted statement and looking to you for agreement or otherwise. A mere incline of your head may be taken as acquiescence, so that this leading statement ends up as *your* quote. You must take control of these situations by stating politely, but firmly: 'Those may be your views, they certainly aren't mine. What *our* company believes should be done in this situation is . . .'

- Don't assume you're the only person the journalist will be talking to.

- Conversely, if you've agreed to an *exclusive* interview, keep it that way. Journalists are very sensitive about their 'scoops'.

- Unless there are some complicated facts involved, which you have every right to check for accuracy – remember that it's tedious and humiliating (and in some cases *very* expensive) for journalists to have to print retractions and apologies – it is unlikely that a print journalist will send you the copy before it goes to print. The ploy of ringing to find out if the journalist needs any further information sometimes gives you a second bite, but don't rely on it.

- If you're pleased with the resulting piece, always write and say so. Conversely, if it does contain factual errors, write a civil letter to the journalist, with a copy to the editor, pointing out the mistakes. Your corrections may not be printed, but if the paper is half-way scrupulous they will at least be logged on the file. The next time someone comes to write about your company and looks you up in the file, he or she will at least start with the right facts.

Telephone

Telephone interviews with the press tend to be much shorter than face-to-face ones and they are beset with traps:

- You can't read any of the body language signals (see Chapter 5).

- You have no idea what the reporter is writing down.

- The conversation tends to be hurried, often forcing you to desert the three principles of confidence, clarity and control.

If a call comes through to you *unscreened*, you have every right to ask the journalist's name, the name of the journal and what the journalist wants to talk about. Explain that you're rather tied up at that precise moment, but that you'll ring right back. Failure to do so will inevitably result in a peeved journalist and probably sour copy. As long as you do phone back, you will have brought yourself valuable thinking time – sufficient breathing space to collect your three main points, talk to your Press Office, and try to anticipate what might be asked.

Such is the power of the telephone, many people have great difficulty in saying 'no' to whoever is on the other end of the line. But there will be occasions when it isn't prudent for you to talk to the press on the phone. In which case remember either:

- to tell the truth and explain that you can't divulge anything at the moment but that they will be the *first* to hear when you can; or . . .

- to suggest that they telephone someone else in the company. Please make sure you warn the individual that a call might be on its way. If that person doesn't want to talk to the journalist, his or her unavailability just *might* deter the enquirer. Remember, the journalist has a deadline and it might be just as easy to get a comment from another source. This approach should be used only as a last resort. Journalists may not be intellectual, but they are *very* perceptive and quickly recognize a rebuff.

Remember in a press interview

- Never let the length of the interview deter you from giving clear, succinct answers.
- Be wary of leading questions.
- Always check that a journalist has recorded your points accurately.
- You are not obliged to take an unscreened call, but you must phone back once you've established the journalist's credentials.
- If you are being interviewed on the phone, try and inject warmth into the voice.
- As you talk, make a note of your key points.
- Don't be afraid to check the facts – better to do so now, rather than later.

What to expect in a group interview

There may well be many occasions on radio and television when you are asked to join a discussion panel. So long as you have exercised your right to know who else will be taking part, these occasions shouldn't present too many problems. If you have the opportunity to meet in the green room or reception before the broadcast, be friendly and by all means introduce yourself, but adopt the pose of listener rather than interlocuter. By so doing, you will pick up some useful indicators as to your opponent's arguments.

Remembering that a producer wants a lively, entertaining programme, don't always feel obliged to catch the chairman's eye before joining in the debate. So long as the discussion doesn't degenerate into a cacophonous shouting match, spontaneous intervention makes for lively broadcasting.

It is also very important, when taking part in a joint discussion, to *listen* actively. Too often, if we're not actually speaking, we tend to let both our minds and our bodies wander. Lapse in concentration manifests itself either as boredom or as distracting, unconscious physical mannerisms, such as slouching, foot-tapping or, even worse, nose-picking.

Remember in a group interview

- Always establish who else is taking part.
- If you have the chance to meet the panel prior to broadcast listen rather than talk.
- You don't always have to go through the chair to make a point.

5 How to conduct a successful interview

When the eyes say one thing and the tongue another, a practised man relies on the language of the first.
Ralph Waldo Emerson, 'Behaviour' from *The Conduct of Life*, 1860

So, you are almost ready for your first media encounter. You've assessed the opposition, anticipated their line of attack, drawn up your own battle plans and reconnoitred the terrain. What you *haven't* yet done is chosen your uniform or put yourself through a dummy run.

Your appearance

There is a great temptation, especially on the *first* visit to a radio or television studio, to alter one's appearance radically. On no account try to do so. Resist the urge to buy a new suit. Vanity inevitably prevails and you'll end up with a size too small. Regular breathing is difficult enough during an interview without the added complication of restricted waist bands. Don't get your hair cut the day before. The shorn look will only add to your sense of vulnerability.

What we're looking for is you at your best. Just because you're about to become public property doesn't mean that your whole personality changes. London taxi drivers, who, if their tales are to be believed, ferry *only* the rich and famous, often remark that so-and-so was 'just like they are on the telly', proving that the most successful communicators retain their identity *whatever* their status.

Television is all about making an *impression*, which is why

120

you choose your wardrobe carefully. On 20 July 1984, Margaret Thatcher appeared on the Michael Aspel show – the first Prime Minister ever to appear on a chat show. Not an Iron Lady in sight. She almost skipped into the studio, wreathed in smiles, hair soft, swathed in a bright pink floating dress. She gushed and cooed throughout the interview, and even told a few jokes. What she was obviously trying to do was to create an impression with the audience of maternal softness.

So what should you do about *your* appearance?

- The clothes you wear for television should suit your own personality and the style of the programme. Don't wear anything that will distract the viewer from what you're saying.

- Certain colours and patterns are out simply because the camera lens can't cope with them. Bold stripes and small checks tend to 'dance' in front of the camera. For many years Sir David Steel, former leader of the Liberal Party, used to wear boldly striped shirts. Perhaps someone told him, as he's now stopped doing so. TV cameras also have difficulty in coping with blocks of very bold colours, so avoid bright red especially. Black and white does disastrous things to the definition of your face.

- If you wear glasses, make sure they're clean and, unless you want to be publicly associated with the Mafia, that they aren't the ones that darken in bright light. Studio lights are very bright and will very quickly affect the colour of your lenses.

- Don't wear clanking jewellery or stuff your top pocket with pens or personal organizers. If your watch is digital, make sure that all bleeping reminders are silenced.

- At the risk of sounding like a tutor from the Lucie Clayton Charm School, make sure you're properly groomed for the occasion. Hair should be clean and tidy, fingernails clean, nail polish unchipped, shoes shining, tights unladdered and socks sufficiently long to prevent the 'NHG' syndrome: when seated, trousers inevitably ride up the leg revealing, if the sock is too short, the 'nasty hairy gap'. Many is the time I have become transfixed by an unsightly expanse of white leg, and totally lost my concentration.

● Because studios are hot, always try and wear a natural material next to your skin. Nylon creates static, and other artificial fibres tend to cling when you sweat. It's sensible to carry a cotton handkerchief with you – useful for the final blowing of the nose and the wiping of clammy hands before going in. It's unlikely that you'll need it when you're in the studio. Perhaps you have noticed how very few people cough or sneeze during an interview?

● Do expect to be made up. Men tend to need it to reduce 'shine' and women to stop their features disappearing. As a television presenter, I always enjoy the make-up session. It provides a temporary lacuna, during which time I begin my relaxation routine (see p. 123).

Practice

However self-conscious you may feel, practice prior to the event always pays dividends. Most firms possess simple video recording equipment and cassette players. Seek out a colleague and get him or her to conduct a mock interview. The lessons you will learn from the playback will be invaluable.

A more long-term approach would be to arrange for yourself and senior management to receive 'media training'. This consists of one or two-day seminars, during which you are subjected to a variety of media experiences. For a session to be really useful, you must take the trainers into your confidence and supply them with as much information about the *negative* aspects of your company as the positive. By so doing, the interviews will be much more relevant and taxing. Because practising journalists will seldom know as much as you do about the subject, it's unlikely you'll be given nearly such a rough ride when you step into the real arena. You will also have overcome certain inhibitions, know a little more about what to expect and might also be rethinking aspects of your company policy.

Relaxation

Confidence comes from being relaxed – which, of course, is the very *last* thing you'll be feeling before you go into the studio. But, if you're to marshal that flow of adrenaline, you have somehow got to convince your body that it's relaxed.

There's no need to go through a whole set of aerobic exercises to achieve the required effect. Discreet tensing and relaxing of certain muscles should do the trick. In each case, keep your breathing deep and regular.

Simply clenching the fists, holding the position for a slow count to five, and then releasing them, will result in a sense of relaxation for the arms and hands. It also helps to mouth silently the word 'relax' several times as you go through the exercise.

Biting your teeth together hard will relax the jaw, just as pushing the tongue against the roof of your mouth will relax the tongue and throat. Again, hold the tensed position for a slow count to five. Raising the eyebrows and frowning, so long as you don't alarm anybody, also helps to relax the facial muscles. Try shrugging your shoulders, clenching your buttocks or tensing your stomach. They will all produce the same desired effect of relaxation.

If you want to try and control a wobbly voice, just before you begin to speak drop your chin. Your voice will be much lower than you expect.

My anxiety level reaches dangerous heights just before I broadcast, but I find that these exercises and the creation of a few minutes 'space' usually quell the urge to quit.

First impressions

According to Graham Lancaster, a first impression is made in:

> One or two seconds. That's how long it takes for people import-
> ant to you to arrive at their opinion of you as a person, or of
> your product or organisation.
> This is not merely a first impression – although it is that as
> well – but their whole opinion. Anything you do or say after
> these first seconds may help strengthen this opinion, or begin
> the long and difficult job of changing it. Just to make things even
> more difficult, research shows how important non-rational
> and emotional factors are in this complex process of opinion
> forming – often outweighing rational assessment.
> (Graham Lancaster, *The 20% Factor*)

Author and psychologist David Lewis adds his two-penny
worth:

> Research has shown that only seven per cent of the meaning
> of any conversation is contained in the words alone; the rest is
> communicated in body talk, in a whole vocabulary, grammar
> and syntax of posture, gesture, gaze and expression.
> (David Lewis, The Secret Language of Success)

Whilst I intend to go into some detail about body language –
or 'non-verbal communication' as it's officially known – it's important for the reader not to become fixated with mannerism.
If your silent language contradicts your verbal one, or your
gestures detract from your message, *then* you should read further
books on the subject. If not, you'll find the following observations will merely enhance your people-watching pleasures.

Assuming that you've followed the preparation guidelines
outlined in Chapter 3, you should by now be leaving make-up
and being led to the studio to meet your interviewer.

There are three key non-verbal acts of communication you
must perform before uttering a word.

- Establish eye contact.
- Smile.

● Shake hands.

Eye contact

We've all experienced conversations with people who look over rather than at you. We've endured the tedium of read speeches and suffered the discomfort of being stared at.

Establish *immediate* eye contact with your interviewer. To do so is your first step towards taking control of the interview. By taking the initiative, you are giving your first non-verbal signal of confidence. It is of course unnatural, and indeed counterproductive, to try and hold eye contact throughout the entire interview. However, a high level of eye contact with the interviewer is essential in the one-to-one interview. This is one of the reasons why it is not advisable to take sheaves of notes with you into the studio.

David Lewis in *The Secret Language of Success* has set out some useful guidelines:

> If you are a man dealing with another male, maintain eye-contact for between 60 and 70 per cent of the time. Anything less is liable to be interpreted as a sign of shiftiness, unease or lack of confidence. Longer gaze, however, will be interpreted as aggressive.
>
> If you are a male dealing with a woman, reduce eye-contact slightly, to around 50 per cent of the exchange. If you are a woman dealing with a man and wish to assert yourself in the situation, use eye-contact around 70 per cent of the time.
>
> To create maximum rapport, be sure to offer eye-contact whenever the other person *starts* talking. This reassures him that you are paying attention ... Remember that the greater attention and interest you can convey by means of appropriately used gaze, the more people will believe you like them and the more liking they will show you in return.

He makes another valid point:

> *Always* break eye contact *downward*, unless it is your deliberate intention to convey a lack of interest in the other person...

This, of course, is precisely what you *don't* want to do.

125

Smiling

I've already mentioned how smiling on radio injects warmth and humanity into the voice. It has the double benefit on television because you are also *seen* to be warm. The warmth of your smile will be reflected in your eyes, which will already have made the vital initial contact. It is very important, if your smile is to come across as sincere, that you mentally convince yourself of the pleasure about to be derived from the exchange. If you don't, the interviewer will see through the deceit and will often misinterpret your nervousness as aggression.

Having established the need to smile, I must emphasize that you should be careful not to overdo it. If you are defending your company's worsening employment record, an ear-to-ear grin won't endear you to either the interviewer or the audience.

Shaking hands

One doesn't need to be a Desmond Morris to recognize the meaning of an outstretched hand. If you can be the *first* to proffer it, you've gained another point in the control stakes.

Before you do 'extend the hand of friendship', make sure it's dry. The only thing worse than a limp handshake is a limp, *damp* handshake. As most people know, our sweat glands respond to temperature changes, producing sweat to cool the body down. But the hand contains papillary sweat glands which produce moisture in response to stress or fear. In a fight or flight situation, our hand not only starts to sweat more, but also grows colder. David Lewis recommends imagining your hand getting warmer, or putting the palm to your face.

I've shaken hands as limp as yesterday's lettuce, and the impression created is very poor indeed. Conversely, I don't like the vice grip, or the pump action or the arm fondle. Keep it simple. Make sure your hand is warm and dry and the shake firm and strong, but not excessively so. If you can manage to tilt your head slightly whilst shaking hands, smiling *and* maintaining eye contact, I'm told that the bonding will be complete.

126

Body language

> He that has eyes to see and ears to hear may convince himself
> that no mortal can keep a secret. If his lips are silent, he chatters
> with his fingertips; betrayal oozes out of him at every pore.
> (Sigmund Freud)

Experienced broadcasters might not always be as well informed
as they ought, but they are extremely perceptive, and they
very often take their cue as to your state of mind not from
what you are saying, but from your body language.

Posture

Whoever designed the studio couch is in the wrong job. It
might make the studio set look cosy and informal, but it will
do nothing for your appearance as it is almost impossible to
sit attractively in one. You inevitably slip forward, you've
nowhere to rest your arms, and the camera angle would give
a stick insect a double chin. If it is your misfortune to have to
conduct your interview from a reclining position, remember
to make sure your feet reach the ground, and try leaning
towards the interviewer.

More serious programmes put their guests on chairs. But
even a studio chair can be a hazard, especially if it swivels.
Swivel chairs are hard to control, and whilst occasional body
movement enhances a performance, appearing to deliver your
lecture from a raft or to conduct an interview from a chair
with a mind of its own doesn't. *You have been warned.*

Desmond Morris has a fascinating theory as to what we're
really doing when we swivel from side to side. All of us are
blessed with the fight or flight instinct and, although not
consciously, are constantly reacting to it during a tension-
inducing interview or lecture. You want to stay and give
your talk, but you'd also like to escape from the intimidating
audience. The struggle between the two imperatives results in
rhythmic swaying from side to side on the platform, or constant
swivelling in your chair.

Whatever seat you're given, find a posture that's comfortable

127

for you. If the seat is too high, get it lowered. If your vision is obscured by the vase of flowers, ask for them to be moved.

The ideal posture is to get your bottom as far back in the seat as possible, and then lean the trunk of your body slightly forward. By so doing, you are giving your interviewer a silent, but effective, signal that you are willing to participate in the conversation. If you're wearing a suit, remember to pull the jacket well down as you take your seat – otherwise it will tend to ride up over your collar.

There is much discussion about whether or not to cross the legs. On the whole, I'd recommend doing so. It adds interesting line to the body and will prevent nervous foot-tapping. For some reason, men look very odd crossing their legs at the ankles, whereas with women it seems quite natural. This probably dates back to Victorian times when it was considered unseemly for women to cross their legs at the knee.

The one seated position which both men *and* women must avoid is the Widow Twankey one. This is where the person slumps in the chair with legs wide apart. Not only is it extremely ungainly, but it rivets the eye on the genitals and completely loses any chance of getting anything other than a sexual message across.

Folding the arms across the chest is a very defensive posture to adopt during an interview, as it literally sets up a barrier between the two parties.

Gesture

I remember once training a chief executive who had been told that during an interview he should 'sit on his hands'. Fortunately, the fashion for stiff, stylized interviews went out years ago. If you are a natural gesticulator, don't let the cameras inhibit you. Used with discretion, gesture is a vital communication tool. It only becomes a burden when it detracts from the verbal message. If gesture doesn't come easily, don't try and force it. A tentative lift of the hand will come across as under-confidence.

It always comes as a shock to see yourself on video for the first time – not only because you won't want to believe that you really *do* look like that, but also because you had no idea that you do so many extraordinary things to your body.

It would probably surprise a balding man to see that he constantly stroked his forehead as if coaxing back hair growth. You might not realize that you bite your lower lip, fiddle with your left ear lobe or jingle the coins in your pocket. These are all unconscious actions, the intensity of which increases with accelerating nervousness. The same rules apply to unconscious gestures, as to conscious ones. If the nervous flicking back of your hair is likely to distract your audience, then stop it.

It's interesting to watch how young children, when they don't want to talk to someone, will cover their mouths with their hands. Quite unconsciously adults will do the same. It often happens at the critical moment in a media training session when a trainee is about to do his or her first interview. As we are going through the preliminaries of voice level, fixing of microphones and so on, as if from nowhere a hand will begin to creep across the mouth.

If you even only *suspect* that you might cover your mouth in stressful circumstances, put a stop to the habit immediately. Mouth covering conveys a silent message of extreme discomfort to the interviewer and, in severe instances, actually prevents your audience hearing what you're saying.

Similarly, although it's hard to prove scientifically, when interviewees start rubbing their nose, people in the media tend to assume that they're lying. Certainly the gesture will alert the interviewer that the interviewee is feeling particularly uncomfortable and might be hiding something.

Again, Desmond Morris has his thoughts as to what may be happening. He suggests that, whereas a child may clamp its hand over its mouth to suppress a lie, this would not be acceptable in adult behaviour. Instead, the hand reaches for the next best thing – the nose – the touching of which also partially covers the mouth. He also observes that even the most experienced liars display an increase in tension at the moment of deception, which can lead to minor physiological changes. The sensitivity of the lining of the nose may be affected, provoking a desire to scratch it. With due respect to Pinocchio, the *length* of one's nose is no indicator of honesty.

129

Confidence

To succeed as an interviewee you must be *confident, clear and in control.*

Because you will know more about your subject than your interviewer, and will have recognized that the interviewer needs you as much as you need him or her, you will already be innately confident about the pending encounter. Your rigorous preparation and practice, and appropriate dress, will also stand you in very good stead. All that remains is to *convey* that confidence, through the interviewer, to your audience.

An interview with the media should be treated as a very intense, albeit brief, love affair. You have got to make your questioner *like* you, and you've got to let the interviewer know, very early on in the relationship, that you're going to sing and dance and make him or her look good in front of the audience. Adopt this technique and the floor is yours. Failure to do so gives rise to either bland or hostile questions.

And don't forget what we've said about flattery. Paying a compliment about the interviewer's programme/article may very well encourage him or her to take a softer line.

The majority of interviewees, if they're honest with themselves, will already be feeling distinctly uncomfortable about the artificiality of the interview. How can you get through in ten seconds to someone you've never met before? Why should you go through the pretence of seduction and flattery?

The only way to overcome such understandable resistance is to treat any media encounter as a *performance.* Your costume is your carefully chosen wardrobe, you've learnt your lines, and you know your audience. You are playing a part, a very important part, but in the final analysis only a part. This distancing approach will enable you to project yourself far more positively. If your *attitude* is right, so too will be your performance.

Confidence is infectious, and needn't necessarily be dependent on good looks. One of my favourite television presenters is bald and overweight, two physical drawbacks I readily forgive because of the man's consummate wit. Clive James *exudes* confidence, clarity and control. The next time you're at a party, seek out the person having the most fun. More often than not it'll be someone with a smile on their face and a confident bearing.

Confidence exerts power. An American TV documentary producer was recently making a programme about street gangs. The leader of a particular gang was a confident 17-year-old, who claimed to make hundreds of dollars each week as a mugger. When asked how he picked his victims, he blithely replied that he looked for isolated people who shuffled along, heads down, eyes averted, and who seemed frightened. Asked whether he would have a go at the producer, his reply was emphatic:

When I first walked into the room, you looked right into my eyes, and then you looked me up and down as if measuring me, to judge if you could take me on in a fight. Those kind of people cause trouble.
(*Reader's Digest*, November 1989)

Confidence makes people feel comfortable. A short while ago, I was given the opportunity of turning the tables on Terry Wogan and interviewing him. When I asked him whether he still felt nervous before his live show, he said:

No, you can't. You mustn't be nervous on television. You mustn't be afraid or apprehensive, because it shows in your eyes. The first thing the viewer looks at is your eyes, and if in there he or she reads fear or apprehension, loathing or terror, then that in turn embarrasses them and they say, 'I can't watch this, it's making me uncomfortable.'

131

Clarity

Jargon is the weed in the garden of language. It's prolific and very difficult to get rid of, but dispose of it you *must* if you're to communicate effectively. The rule is very simple. If the layman won't understand it, don't use it.

We're all guilty of using jargon, sometimes as a genuine shorthand. Everybody *inside* the BBC knows that DG refers to the Director-General and an FM is a floor manager. But as an outsider, *you* wouldn't know that. As far as you're concerned, FM is a radio wave band.

In speech, jargon creeps in as a cover for intellectual inferiority. Because communication at any level exposes us to the possibility of ridicule, the more we depersonalize our language, the less likely we are to be found out.

During a recent media training session, the managing director of a company was asked why his factory was closing:

> The factory will be closed because we have overcapacity within the industry. There has been a downturn in the industry over the last ten years that has resulted in us having more capacity than we need. The location is not near to the market place which we serve, and consequently the factory will have to close.

How much more effective it would have been to say:

> This is one of the saddest days in the history of our factory. But, as you probably know, the fact that our industry has been declining over the last ten years and that our factory is too far away means we have no alternative but to close.

Here's another example. A sales director is being quizzed about the availability of the products in his catalogue:

> We always launch our products in the catalogue prior to them being installed in the stores, because a purchase decision for the consumer is a decision that does take a long time – we're not in the *small ticket value market*.

132

What he *really* meant was that, because his products are considered luxury items, and are expensive, consumers take quite a long time making up their minds, which is why the goods might be in the catalogue before appearing in the stores. Two of my favourite examples of jargon are the marketing director telling his sales team that he is looking for an ability to flex the product and an underwear manufacturer who referred to his product as apparel garments.

We all have our pet irritations. Why say 'at this moment in time' when 'at the moment' or 'now' is sufficient? 'Situation' is another popular irrelevance:

I'm afraid you can't speak to him at the moment, he's in an interview situation. [I'm sorry, you can't speak to him at the moment, he's interviewing somebody.]

The British love their euphemisms:

This really is rather a poor show. [You're fired.]

He's just popped out for a moment. [He's late and we don't know when he'll be in.]

I'm afraid our accounts department is closed for the afternoon. [I have no intention of paying you this week.]

We also have a tendency to use complicated rather than simple words:

thought provoking: interesting
problematic: difficult
indefatigable: hard-working
effervescent: lively

Always go back to that image of the intelligent twelve-year-old. Will he or she understand what you're talking about?

Now that you've stripped out the jargon and the cliches from your conversation, you can get to work on developing the art of introducing *colour* and *anecdote*. The constraints of time make the introduction of the latter quite difficult, but it is always a good idea to have at least a couple of stories to hand before any interview. People will remember a story far more easily than statistics or a shopping list of facts. It worked in the Bible so why shouldn't it work for you?

You should occasionally substitute *humour* for colour. A witty observation to illustrate a point will relax your interviewer and entertain your audience.

You are not likely to speak with clarity if you are under the influence of alcohol. For this reason you should not accept any alcoholic drinks before the show, although you should ask for liquid refreshment of some kind.

Control

With the odds seemingly stacked so heavily against you, the hardest part of getting to grips with an interview is *believing* that you can take control. Bearing in mind the obstacles, it requires a huge psychological leap to move from the defensive to the offensive, particularly when a journalist seems to like you best when you're submissive.

Journalists also seem to hold all the cards:

- They are assertive and opinionated.
- They are at ease with the environment, and you're not.
- They make you think they can read your mind.
- They ask the questions, you provide the answers.
- They won't report you accurately.
- They are out to get you.
- They are only interested in bad news.

Some of the above assertions are indeed true. But not only can they all be dealt with, they also only tell *half* the story.

THEY ARE ASSERTIVE AND OPINIONATED

There are very few journalists who approach an interview with a completely open mind. Like you, they are subject to all kinds of influences: their own or their paper's political beliefs, their education, their personal experiences and so on. The journalist's opinion is based on these experiences, will always form the 'angle' to the story, and without the 'angle' any journalist would find it difficult to structure an interview. Things tend to go wrong when the journalist, despite everything you're saying, seems determined to make the story match his or her views rather than yours. How to take steps to prevent this happening will be discussed in a moment.

It is certainly the case that many journalists, especially the ones who work for the tabloid press or who cover politics, are assertive and aggressive – the former because they often trespass morally, and the latter because they believe they are crusaders for truth. Much of their assertiveness is sheer *bluff*. They want a reaction from you and they think they'll get one by pushing you to the limits. If you are in control, this tactic will inevitably fail. They will end up huffing and puffing, while you remain calm and collected. Be far more wary of quietly spoken interviewers. They quickly lull you into a sense of spurious familiarity, which lowers your defences.

THEY ARE AT EASE WITH THE ENVIRONMENT, AND YOU'RE NOT

We're all much more comfortable in a familiar setting. But it shouldn't matter where the interview takes place, so long as you remember to concentrate your attention on the interviewer and not on any of the distractions around you.

THEY MAKE YOU THINK THEY CAN READ YOUR MIND

Interviewers seem to have a knack of mentally disrobing an interviewee and getting at the naked truth. But remember, if they do, it's more likely to be by *chance* than design. They might be able to read your body language, but they can't read your mind. Your hesitation might suggest discomfort, but it will be instinct, not knowledge, that drives them to press you. You know more about your subject than they ever will – you've done your homework and you're ready to make your three points.

135

THEY ASK THE QUESTIONS, YOU PROVIDE THE ANSWERS

Your attitude towards an interviewer is the key to taking control successfully. The question must be treated purely as a catalyst for *your* ideas. Remember, you are there to tell your story, not to endorse the interviewer's half-baked theory. Unfortunately, politicians have so blatantly abused the skill of turning an interview to their own advantage that they have lost all credibility. But because most of you will have had very little media experience, it is most unlikely that your responses will come across as either calculated or evasive. You will simply give your audience confidence in you because you will seem to be in control. But it must be stressed again that, unless you know *beforehand* what you want to say, you may be forced back into the defensive role of trying to answer the question.

I'm often asked whether it's a useful tactic to turn the tables and ask the interviewer a question. Unless you're feeling very confident, it's a dangerous ploy. Even if they suspect it may not be so, media folk like to think that it's their show and they are the ones in control. Publicly challenging their assumed authority usually results in a stinging dressing-down:

> I hate to remind you, Mr Smith, but it is *my* job to ask the questions and *yours* to answer...

Only the most foolhardy would try and pursue that line.

THEY WON'T REPORT YOU ACCURATELY

Remember, unless you put your points across clearly and succinctly, there is every chance that you *will* be misquoted. At the end of an interview, especially with a journalist, take control and ask him or her to read back to you certain passages where you suspect misunderstandings may have arisen. Don't be afraid to repeat some of your unsolicited points. So often, the last thing on the journalist's mind is the first thing to appear in print.

Despite all you do to keep the initiative there is no guarantee that the interviewer won't misrepresent you. It comes back again to the human element. You may be lucky and give an interview to a hard-working, well-informed professional. On the other hand, you may encounter someone with a bias impossible to budge. Don't become over-sensitive about being misrepresented. A misquote in an article might wound your ego, but it will be quickly forgotten by everyone else.

Of course, if the article or programme is likely to do *permanent* damage, then you must do something about it. Procedures for this will be dealt with in Chapter 7.

THEY ARE OUT TO GET YOU

Journalists are fond of quoting Harry Truman's advice, 'If you can't stand the heat, get out of the kitchen', in defence of their sometimes maverick approach to news stories. Hopefully you won't find yourself in Elton John's or Koo Stark's situation.

If you can avoid the unscrupulous, you will find that most journalists are not 'out to get you'. They want a story that's colourful and lively, and that will please readers, viewers and editors alike. If you can serve it up with a dash of confidence as well, you'll go into their little black book and be asked back. If, on the other hand, you come across as weak and dithering, you're quite likely to trigger their 'killer instinct' and they *will* get you.

THEY ARE ONLY INTERESTED IN BAD NEWS

Let's face it, bad news is exciting, especially news of a human catastrophe. Reading about a train crash in which you *could* have been involved momentarily restores your own faith in life. We will come to controlling bad news in Chapter 6.

But what about controlling good news? What's the point of hammering away with news of your factory extension, if you know your local paper is only interested in redundancies?

Persistence, in any walk of life, eventually pays off. Because you've been regularly supplying your local paper with helpful ideas for stories and information about your company, even though nothing may have made the printed page, at least the staff on the paper are aware of your existence. This means, when they next need comment from a local industrialist, they are more likely to come to you than one of your competitors.

You should by now have broken the psychological belief barrier. You *can* take control of an interview.

Techniques

Always remember, when giving an interview, that the interviewer's goal is the same as yours – a good programme or article. Their only advantage is their familiarity with the technology; their disadvantage is that they are usually under-prepared and will certainly have only a fraction of your knowledge.

You've got to be *confident, clear, and in control*, even if the questions are ill-constructed, hostile or stupid. It is sometimes more difficult to respond engagingly to a bored interviewer than it is to a barracking one. Although the physical techniques of giving a good interview are similar to those required when speaking in public, some people, because they are reacting to a question rather than self-starting, find the former a much less daunting experience.

Pitch

The tremulous voice is an instant give-away of nervous anxiety, as is the high-pitched squeak. The pitch of our voice is controlled by the amount of air passing across the vocal cords. The more nervous we become, the shallower and faster our breathing, and the higher the pitch of the voice. A falsetto voice, especially in a man, does *not* inspire confidence.

If you are to control your voice, first you must learn to control your breathing, and also your posture – it is impossible to breathe correctly if the position of your body is restricting the flow of air into your lungs. Before you practise breathing, check your posture when you are sitting down. Do you slump? Do you thrust your head backwards when you go to speak? If you do, then you are off to a bad start. In any interview, always check that you are sitting straight, and that you don't throw your head around as you speak.

It's a good idea to think about breathing long before you find yourself in an interview. Lie down on the floor, with your feet apart and flat to the floor, and with your knees to the ceiling. You may feel more comfortable with a book under your head. Try to relax completely, not just your leg and stomach muscles but also the muscles of your face, and make sure your jaw is not tight. Then, think about your breathing. Breathe regularly and slowly. As you breathe in, you should feel your diaphragm rise and your rib-cage expand. Make sure that the air is filling all of your lungs, not just the top part. Try to feel your back expand as well as your chest.

After performing your deep-breathing exercises for about ten minutes, try humming as you exhale. You will find that the sound is surprisingly deep. Then stand up slowly, and recite a poem or rehearse your three points. The pitch of your voice will be lower and more controlled than before. Although initially you may have been sceptical about the value of such an exercise, you have made the first step towards realizing that we *can* control our voices.

Another useful exercise is intercostal diaphragmatic or 'rib-reserve' breathing. Fill your lungs – you'll feel the diaphragm rising and the rib-cage expanding – and, just as you feel you've inhaled enough air, take another gulp (the reserve). By taking in far more air than usual, you're unlikely to run out mid-sentence and the pitch of your voice will improve.

If you can find the time, practise these techniques regularly. If you can manage to correct bad breathing permanently, your voice will improve dramatically. The Victorian actor-manager Henry Irving had a favourite party trick of filling his lungs and reciting Hamlet's 'To be or not to be?' three times. Although your breath control may never be *quite* that good, always take a few deep breaths before an interview, check your posture, and try to remember to breathe properly at all times.

Pace

Have you noticed how nervous people either become agonizingly slow or absurdly fast in their delivery? Neither makes for compulsive listening.

As well as learning to control the speed of your speech, you must become aware of the need to vary the pace and intonation. Generally, when you're wanting to emphasize a point, it's good to slow down and either raise or lower the voice. Relatively unimportant information can be delivered fairly fast.

Intonation, or modulation of the voice, is an acquired skill, but it's useful to remember that a sentence finished on an upward inflection will denote unfinished business, and a downward one usually completes an idea.

Pause

A pause, at the appropriate moment, can greatly enhance the emphasis of a sentence.

We will *not* give in [pause] ever.

See how much more effective this sounds than the conventional approach, without a pause:

We will never give in.

Answering the question

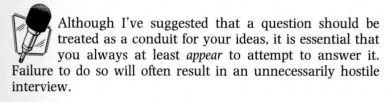 Although I've suggested that a question should be treated as a conduit for your ideas, it is essential that you always at least *appear* to attempt to answer it. Failure to do so will often result in an unnecessarily hostile interview.

Content and length

A question must *never* be answered with a bald 'yes' or 'no'. To do so guarantees a collapse of the fragile relationship between interviewer and interviewee. Nor must your answer contain more than *one* point. How often has your heart sunk on hearing someone limbering up for a three-point answer? And what mirth when only two points can be recalled.

There's a temptation to be more expansive with the press than on radio or television. Adopt the same rigorous discipline with all three media. No answer should be longer than 60 seconds, preferably 30. Only one main point should be made at a time. Substitute an image for a statistic, and never talk in lists.

An ill-prepared interviewee will always have two stabs at answering a question. The first part of the answer will be the rehearsal, followed, the interviewee hopes, by a clearer statement. If you do this during a live interview, you'll certainly never be asked back. If you do it during a recorded one, the chances are all of you will end up on the cutting room floor.

Acknowledgement and action

Most answers fall into two parts: the *acknowledgement* and the *action*:

> That's quite right, it has been a problem [acknowledgement], but, as our recent figures show, we now lead the field [action].

Problematic questions can often be fielded by an extended acknowledgement:

> That's an interesting question but, first, can I put it into perspective? [briefly please]

> I'm glad you asked me that, because it brings me to a point I've been wanting to make.

> You're quite right to ask me that, but I think what is perhaps *more* interesting is...

141

I don't have the precise details about that, but what I *do* know is...

I'm often asked that...

What I *think* you mean by the question is...

These bridging phrases will only help if you know what you want to say. If you *do*, they will buy you precious thinking time to recall one of your points which it is very unlikely the interviewer will ask you.

Confrontation

Don't be afraid to deflect a direct question to make your point. Equally, be prepared to answer the *same* question next time around. If you feel you have genuinely gone as far as you are able with a question, have the confidence to politely, but firmly, tell your interviewer so. Similarly, don't allow yourself to be bullied into divulging sensitive or confidential information. Try using a little guile.

Interviewer: Mr Gross, just what were your profit margins last year?

Mr Gross: [Small smile] I don't think my accountants would be too happy if I divulged that information. What I am able to tell you is that our turnover is up and we've added twenty more people to our wage bill.

The negative trigger

There are certain words and phrases that should be avoided in answers as they ring automatic warning bells in a perceptive interviewer's ear:

> behind schedule
> disappointing
> poor performance
> satisfactory
> hazardous

reasonable
uncertain
unresolved

Truth

If you don't know something, *don't* make it up:

> I'm sorry, I don't have that information on me, but if your caller would like to phone my office in the morning, I can certainly let her have details by then.

And *don't* lie. You may not be caught the first, second or even third time, but once you are it will be a long, hard haul back to credibility. And some of you won't make it. Remember John Profumo and his lie to the House of Commons? It cost him his job.

The last word

Some unprincipled presenters will try and turn the knife at the end of the interview, in the mistaken belief that you won't have the temerity to challenge them. If, in your opinion, a presenter does try and close the interview with a snide unfair remark, you *must* strike back, even though you think the programme may be over. There's always time for a five-second:

> Now you *know* that's not the case.

Remember, it's the last image that the viewer or listener often takes away with them, so you had better make sure it's in your favour.

Product mentions

If you're hard-nosed, you'll mention your company as many times as you can. If you want to be asked back, you'll be more discerning. There are no fixed rules, but generally if the presenter mentions your company in the introduction and sign-off and you bring it in once, you won't incur the wrath of either the BBC or the IBA. A certain quid pro quo exists between presenter and guest. In exchange for bringing a lively story to the station, the presenter will obligingly credit you, and not object to you adding your own bit of self-promotion.

The party's over

Appearing on radio or television, or being interviewed by the press, can be a traumatic experience, and there is an understandable desire, once you think it's over, to let your guard down.

Resist the temptation to turn away from the interviewer and look into a camera. Your apparent disengagement will look at best rude, at worst foolish. And beware of expressing relief – it can have dire consequences.

Picture the scene. You think you've come to the end of a pre-recorded interview and turn to your interviewer expressing heartfelt relief that he'd not taken a particular line of questioning. Unbeknownst to you, the programme director hears your conversation in his control room and decides to act:

> Mr Davies, that was a good interview, thank you. I'm sorry to say, we've hit a technical hitch and the recording is faulty. Do you mind *terribly* doing it again?

Of course you don't mind – it'll probably be easier second time around. How were you to know you'd been set up – that there

144

was *no* fault on the original tape? You obligingly cross the studio floor ready to re-record the interview. This time the first question homes straight in on the *very* subject you didn't want to discuss. And why did it happen? Because you assumed everything was 'off', and that somehow made you safe. *Nothing* is sacred in a studio.

Never assume the camera or microphones are switched off until you are told.

Out of control

To the delight of most audiences, Members of Parliament are prone, from time to time, to lose control. What causes these sudden emotional outbursts we'll never know; after all, politicians should be masters at handling difficult interviews. What we know is that displays of lack of control are treated with derision rather than sympathy.

James Naughtie, a respected reporter on the BBC Radio 4 programme *The World at One*, had arranged to conduct a pre-recorded 'down the line' interview with Neil Kinnock. He asked the Labour leader what his plans would be to bring down interest rates. Kinnock allegedly replied:

> Yes, look Jim, they are making a God awful mess of the economy. They are about to slaughter it and I'm not going to sit on this programme and have a bloody WEA lecture on what the Labour alternatives might be in three years time. For Christ's sake, we are the Opposition, they are the Government. They have cocked it up totally. I'm not going to sit here and be bloody quizzed on the alternatives. He is the Chancellor of the Exchequer.
> (*Evening Standard*, 26 May 1989)

The interview, although never broadcast, was leaked to the press and appeared under the damaging headline: 'REVEALED: THE AMAZING BBC RECORDING OF LABOUR LEADER'S OUTBURST OF SWEARING'.

It is not clear whether Kinnock's words were part of the preamble to the interview or the interview itself, but what the incident shows is that you *never* say anything unguarded in front of a microphone. By losing control, Neil Kinnock:

- lost a valuable opportunity to tell the population how his party would bring down interest rates;
- could have dented his reputation as a potential Prime Minister.
- had to endure his outburst being inflamed by the press.

No one ever won an argument by losing self-control.

Remember

- Always look smart and tidy, but don't change your appearance.
- Avoid bold stripes, checks and gashes of red, white or black.
- Don't wear clanking jewellery or photochromatic spectacles.
- *No alcohol* until after the programme.
- Practise, practise, practise.
- First impressions are the most lasting.
- Be aware of the importance of eye contact and gesture.
- Avoid jargon, but use example, anecdote and colour.
- Control your answers by using pitch, pace and pause.
- Don't let your answers ramble.
- Never try and answer a question in three parts.
- Always avoid the monosyllabic 'yes' or 'no' answer.
- Never make something up and don't lie outright.
- Make sure you have the last word if the interviewer tries to put you down.
- Never walk out.

PART III
DIVORCE

6 How to deal with a crisis

It's old fashioned thinking to feel that the less you say the less the matter will be reported. Of course, the converse is the case, because even if you don't say anything or make a statement, there are plenty of other people around who will.
Michael Bishop, Chairman of British Midland Airways, talking on *The Media Show*, Channel 4, 29 January 1989

When we asked them what the procedure was for such an emergency, they said: 'This sort of thing never happens.'
ITN News, 6 March 1987, at the Headquarters of Townsend Thoresen European Ferries, after the sinking of *The Herald of Free Enterprise* at Zeebrugge.

Your nightmare crisis is a dream made in heaven for a journalist and, if not properly handled, will inevitably be distorted and worsened.

No industry is immune from crisis. Fires, crashes, sinkings, redundancies, poisonings, break-ins, takeovers, strikes, industrial espionage – they all come under the crisis umbrella.

If we are all so susceptible, why is it that so few companies have invested any time or money in establishing emergency procedure plans? Just as most organizations give scant attention to the preparation of non-hostile interviews, so they seem to adopt the same *laissez-faire* attitude towards dealing with the inevitable media attention that follows a crisis.

It's a combination of naivety and indolence:

Well, if it happens, we'll deal with it somehow.

Take that attitude at your peril. By the time a crisis strikes it will be too late to start planning how to deal with it. How are you going to cope with a baying pack of journalists outside your front door on a Sunday morning, trying to get a comment from you, your wife *and* your children?

149

When the news breaks that stocks of your baby-food have been tampered with, they won't be trying to fix up an appointment with you through your secretary, they will be there *on your doorstep*. If the story warrants it, journalists will wait *days* in the hope of catching you off your guard. Although 'chequebook journalism' is generally decried, it does go on. It only takes one dissatisfied employee to take the bait and give a damaging picture of events.

For many, the way to lessen the magnitude of a crisis is to try and avoid the media altogether. This technique might sometimes work but, on the whole, it is far better to deal openly, swiftly and honestly with the problem.

Taking my own advice never to impart more than three ideas at one sitting, there are three important aspects to crisis management:

● anticipation
● preparation
● execution

Anticipation

Sometime in the history of your company, there is bound to be a moment when you'll find yourself having to take a *defensive* stance towards the media. If you haven't taken the trouble to anticipate the occasions when this might occur, you will be caught off guard and will not give of your best.

Draw up a list of the circumstances that might attract crisis media attention. They could include:

● redundancies
● poor company results
● damaging publicity on a consumer programme
● product re-calls
● fatality at the factory
● union feud

- staff walk-out
- fires/explosions/emissions/floods/collapses

It might make for depressing reading, but at least your head will be out of the sand and you will have taken the first essential step towards effective crisis management.

Preparation

Having identified your company's areas of vulnerability, your next task is to appoint a working party, charged with the job of drawing up an emergency procedures plan.

Graham Lancaster, Chairman of the public relations consultancy Biss Lancaster Plc, suggests the following compositions:

> The group might include someone from Personnel (access to personnel records may be necessary in emergencies); from Production (safety or quality issues); the Company Secretary (legal and insurance matters), the Office Services Manager (word processors, telexes, computers, may all need to be accessed); and Marketing (retailers may need to be contacted if it is some kind of poison threat, the bar codes and sell-by dates and any on-pack information may help isolate those items which may need taking off the shelves).

Just as all government ministry press offices are staffed 24 hours a day (including weekends), so you should be prepared to draw up a duty roster of personnel able to react swiftly to a situation the moment it breaks.

Make sure that each member of the team has the contact numbers of every other member and that the elected spokesperson is contactable at all times by bleeper.

151

The company spokesperson

On the whole, the media would rather have a quotable comment from an office junior than a string of meaningless cliches from the Chairman. Ideally, of course, they want the Chairman talking to them in *their* language.

ITN reporter Joan Thirkettle cites Michael Bishop, Chairman of British Midland Airways, as exemplifying the way to deal with the media during a crisis:

> Michael Bishop was at home when he was told the news of the crash of the Boeing 737 on the M1 on the evening of 8 January 1989. He went to the scene immediately, and instantly made himself available to the press.
>
> The way he handled the tragedy was exemplary and serves as a valuable lesson to others who may find themselves having to deal with a similar situation.
>
> 1   He didn't shrink the horror of the event. His humanity prevailed and the press could see he was genuinely distressed.
> 2   He wasn't in the least defensive. He clearly cared deeply about the plight of friends and relatives, was ready to shoulder responsibility should that prove necessary, and was deeply concerned that everything should be done as quickly as possible to discover the cause of the crash.
> 3   Possibly the most important point of all – he didn't hide or issue meaningless statements. He was there!

Joan was not as impressed at the handling of some of the other disasters that occurred around that time:

> When the PAN AM Jumbo crashed at Lockerbie, it took a very long time to get any satisfactory statement from PAN AM. Reporters were constantly referred to the Head Office in America, and their lines were consistently engaged. PAN AM did eventually issue a statement, but it was singularly lacking in compassion and humanity – perhaps it's the problem of dealing with large conglomerates; there is never a figurehead who is immediately identifiable with that company. As a result it's impossible to get the human angle.

Procedure document

Commenting generally on handling a crisis, Graham Lancaster suggests that the next step after selecting your spokespeople is to prepare a procedure document:

> An incident report form should be drawn up, which should be used as soon after the incident as possible by everyone involved, to log events and actions taken.
>
> Problems frequently happen at night, at weekends and during the holidays. One of the first requirements will be to set up an operations room, and this will need full administrative and secretarial support facilities – the switchboard will need manning and special lines dedicated to the incident room (during a major crisis, an ordinary switch board would be swamped). Typists will be required, along with access to the electronically stored data; refreshments and petty cash may be called upon; keys to locked departments and storage areas should be available. The operations room may well need to be open for 24 hours a day, so staff replacements will be needed.

Dummy run

Dummy runs are time-consuming and usually have to take place at weekends. But they are the *only* way to ascertain how your organization would react to a crisis. The lessons learnt from the exercise could be invaluable:

- Have we chosen the right spokesperson?
- Does senior management need a quick course in computer access?
- Where can we find helpers to staff the switchboard?
- Who will speak to the media before our Chief Executive comes on the scene?

Execution

The ideal way to handle an emergency is *automatically*. Rigorous training will trigger the right response.

Although no two disasters are ever the same, there are two golden rules:

- You must be honest.
- You must be efficient.

Honesty

As Richard Nixon found to his cost, there is no point in trying to lie your way out of a crisis. You may not be rumbled the first, second or even third time, but the odds are shortening and so is your nerve.

There is, of course, a subtle difference between lying and the careful selection of the information you wish to impart. Remember, it's your subject and you're in control – or at least you will be if you've taken the trouble to anticipate and prepare for a crisis.

On the whole, journalists only get really aggressive when they think you're hiding something. They are *far* more likely to be sympathetic if you try and deal with the facts as you see them. Even if the story is potentially damaging, you will at least come across as honest and caring, and with any luck you'll be treated as a one-day wonder.

There's always the danger during a crisis that you're going to say something unguarded, simply to 'get them off your back'. A simple way out of this potential mine-field is to issue a statement to the press saying that you expect to be in a position to provide more information whenever you think reasonable. This is the one time when you can legitimately give a 'no comment' reply:

Ladies and gentlemen, as I'm sure you'll appreciate, it would be irresponsible of me to make any comment right now. Our main concern is with our two employees in hospital, which, if

154

you'll excuse me, is where I am now going. *As soon as the situation become a little clearer we will be issuing a statement.*

Reality

We've already talked about the need, when preparing for a crisis, to have an established crisis procedure. Graham Lancaster believes that many a crisis is exacerbated by a failure to face reality:

> Good intentions, however genuine, are nothing like enough. If the story breaks at four o'clock on a Friday afternoon, you can't call a board meeting, issue a committee-written statement late in the evening and expect to see your good intentions reflected by the media.
>
> Equally, you can't push an inexperienced or untrained 'company spokesman' on to the radio or TV or to a hastily called and badly run press conference, and achieve a fair representation of your situation in the media.
>
> If you think you'll get an easier ride than most because, over the years, you've nurtured some good press contacts, then you're in for a shock. What you will more than likely find is that the story is a news-desk one, being put together by whoever the News Editor has available. They will know little, or nothing, about you, other than whatever may be lurking in their library cuttings files, and, because they will be working to very tight deadlines, probably won't have the time or inclination to contact their specialist reporters.
>
> It gets worse. The news-desk people won't seem at all like that friendly specialist with whom you had a long lunch a few months ago. They will be very direct, will either ask you probing questions at the very heart of the matter, or make assumptions which show complete ignorance of how your business operates.
>
> They will be in a hurry, will brusquely cut short any flannel, and if they don't think they are getting anywhere with *you*, will probably demand to speak to your Chairman or Managing Director.
>
> You will interpret this as rudeness, as an insult. But it isn't. The journalist understands the limitations on you to speak, and

simply wants to get a speedy answer to his questions from someone. Remember that the main motivations of any journalist in this situation are twofold.

First, he or she has to make sure they get at least as much of the story as their competitors. If not, they will be in real trouble with their Editor.

Secondly, what they really want, just as they do when they attend a press conference, is either to find a new angle to the story or to unearth more information than their competitors. All this does not necessarily mean that they want to do you down or just generate 'bad news' headlines. Most journalists are just as happy with a story about 'This is what went wrong, this is how we are solving it.' Consumer writers like 'victories'. They like to be able to say, 'We spotted this problem, raised it and we are pleased to say that, thanks to us, the firm has put it right.'

Advice for the spokesperson

Even though you're dealing with a crisis, you still have rights and you should not be bullied into abandoning them.

A useful tip to remember is your right to prohibit filming areas of your establishment. If somewhere is private, tell them. Just in case someone disregards your request, make sure that a member of your team accompanies a film crew around the premises. Be wary of being filmed in an unflattering environment. If you're answering questions about an accident, it won't look good if you're filmed next to a ladder with broken rungs.

Don't take the entire media on to your shoulders. At difficult times, you'll need support. Make sure there's always someone in the background to keep an eye on you and to make a note of what you said. You won't remember either the questions or the answers.

Don't allow yourself to be hectored. It's all too easy to be drawn into a slanging match. You won't win, nor will it do your company's image any good.

Always consider whether you can legitimately broaden what has happened to you in an industry issue, even a national one, to deflect some of the flak from yourself. You might refer to your trade association, a government department, the adequacy or otherwise of national safety standards or testing regulations. When it becomes an industry-wide issue, the damage to your company or product could well be lessened. It could have happened to any of your competitors – that's the message you want to get across.

You might, if you're feeling really bullish, go on the attack and use your misfortune as a platform to call for higher standards or even a change in the law.

There are some key components to your crisis interview, *whatever* questions you are asked:

- Express concern and sympathy for anyone affected.
- Reassure everyone that the matter is being or will be thoroughly investigated.
- Reaffirm your company's excellent safety/hygiene/employment record.
- Always point out that your standards are well above the statutory minimum.
- Never speculate on the cause of the problem.
- Never admit blame or negligence.
- Never commit your company to compensation.

Remember

- Always anticipate.
- Always prepare for a crisis, however much you hope it may never happen.
- Hold occasional dress rehearsals.
- At the time of a crisis, always express sympathy and concern.
- Reassure everyone that the matter is being thoroughly investigated.
- Reaffirm your company's safety/hygiene/employment record.
- Never speculate as to the cause of the problem.
- Never admit to blame or negligence.
- Never commit your company to binding liability.
- Always be honest.
- Always be efficient.
- Always field the best spokesperson for the occasion.

7 Fighting back

Tolerance is a tremendous virtue, but the immediate neighbours of
tolerance are apathy and weakness.
Sir James Goldsmith, *The Listener*, 1979

Until you've been on the receiving end of inaccurate reporting,
it's difficult to imagine the distress it can cause. Fortunately, for
most of us, the mistakes or misrepresentations about ourselves
aren't sufficiently severe to warrant complaint.

Sometimes, the misprint can even be amusing. When asked
by the *Observer* Media Editor to comment on the style of BBC
Radio 3's presenters, I described many of them sounding 'som-
nambulant'. Imagine my surprise to discover the next morning
that I had referred to them sounding 'as if they are broadcasting
from an ambulance'. Should I have complained and insisted
on a correction? I don't think so. I merely wrote a humorous
note to the Media Editor pointing out the misunderstanding,
to which he responded with profuse apologies and a promise
to de-wax his ears. By both of us acting sensibly, a potentially
hostile situation was prevented and a mutual respect established.

However, there are going to be times when you *should* and
must formally complain, particularly if an article or a television
or radio programme contains information that:

● is grossly incorrect;
● could adversely affect your business;
● seriously damage your reputation.

Prevention

It is far better, and cheaper, either to make sure the journalist gets the facts right in the first place or, if not, to correct them on the spot.

On the whole, the press has a poor reputation for accuracy. But, as I've said before, it's wrong to assume that the blame is all on their side. Remember, journalists will be coming to you with two grave disadvantages: lack of knowledge and a deadline. Unless you steer them clearly and smoothly through the interview, don't be surprised if you're misquoted.

We've already dealt with the need to remind a journalist of your three main points at the end of the conversation. Don't be afraid, either, to ask the journalist to read back some of the other quotes that he or she has taken. By so doing, you'll probably endorse your points rather than those of the journalist. Remember, too, to be wary of apparent tacit agreement to a journalist's statement. Silence doesn't mean denial. If there is to be a lot of factual detail in the article, it will be in *both* your interests to check the copy before it goes to press. And, finally, always try and find out when the article will appear.

The same degree of initiative in a radio or television studio could also avoid the necessity of time-consuming complaints. By making sure that you know what you're talking about, that you've exercised your rights and that you've done your homework, you lessen the chances of other people getting it wrong.

Preventing publication or broadcast

If you have got wind of something about to be published or broadcast that is likely to be injurious, you should immediately seek the advice of a solicitor who may well be able to get an injunction to stop it appearing. Specialist advice is needed in these circumstances. If you don't find the appropriate person by personal recommendation, contact the **Law Society (113**

Chancery Lane, London WC2A 1PL, telephone: 071–242 1222) for advice.

Codes of conduct

It takes courage and tenacity to try and get your own back on the media and, judging from the brief apologies that sometimes preface a programme or appear lost in a page of dense newsprint, it might not seem worth the effort and heartache.

However, it is worth bearing in mind that radio, press and television do have certain standards to which they are supposed to adhere. Both the BBC and the IBA publish guidelines. Although going some way towards protecting the individual, these contain many subjective concepts:

... essential to establish the credibility and authority of the story ...

... all reasonable care taken to establish the facts ...

... in the public interest ...
(IBA Television Programme Guidelines)

With regard to conducting interviews, especially for current affairs and documentary programmes, the IBA states:

Each current affairs or documentary programme dealing with matters of political or industrial controversy, or relating to current public policy, should normally attempt to be impartial in itself. This does not mean that balance is required in any simple mathematical sense of equal time or an equal number of lines being given to each relevant viewpoint. It requires, for instance, that the programme should not be slanted by the concealment of relevant facts, or by misleading emphasis, nor should investigation turn into a case for the prosecution or defence or into a kind of trial by television.

In addition to interviews being subject to the normal general

161

requirements of fairness and impartiality, the IBA also requires:

(a) that an interviewee chosen as a representative of an organized group is in a position to speak on behalf of others involved.

(b) that, whether the interview is recorded or live, the interviewee has been made adequately aware of the format, subject matter and purpose of the programme to which he or she has been invited to contribute, and the way in which his or her contribution is likely to be used.

(c) that the interviewee has been told the identity and intended role of any other proposed participant in the programme.

There is, not surprisingly, a caveat to the above:

if *exceptional* circumstances require departure from these usual practices, they should be in consultation with the IBA in advance.

The IBA's guidance as regards edited material is also quite illuminating:

to minimise risk of misunderstanding, or even resentment, the Producer should tell the interviewee that the recording will be much longer than the edited version used in the programme … care should be taken to ensure that the shortened version of the interview does not misrepresent the interviewee's contribution.

Due weight should be given to any qualifying remarks that may perhaps weaken the force of an answer, but to which the interviewee is likely to attach importance.

There is no justification for picking out a brief extract to support a particular line of argument to which the interviewee does not himself subscribe without qualification.

The *context* in which extracts from a recorded interview are used is also important. It is quite defensible to run together a number of different answers by different contributors to the same question. But an interview should not be edited so as to appear by juxtaposition to associate a contributor with a line of argument which he would probably not accept and on which he is given no opportunity to comment in the programme.

The IBA's guidelines on the invasion of privacy advise on the sensitive issue of recorded telephone conversations:

> interviews or conversations conducted by telephone should normally not be recorded for inclusion in a programme or in the course of preparation for a programme, unless the interviewer has identified himself or herself as speaking on behalf of an Independent Television company seeking information to be used in a programme ... and the interviewee has given consent to the use of the conversation.

As with other aspects of its guidelines, the IBA gives examples when its code of conduct needn't necessarily apply. On the controversial issue of the use of concealed microphones and cameras, the IBA states that:

> The use of hidden microphones and cameras to record individuals who are unaware that they are being recorded is acceptable only when it is clear that the material so acquired is essential to establish the credibility and authority of the story, and when the story itself is equally clearly of important public interest.

It also suggests that the responsibility of balancing the needs of truth and the desire for compassion when reporting scenes of human suffering and distress lies with the individual programme producer.

Despite the fact that the newspaper industry is regulated by the Press Council, most of Britain's national newspapers now adhere to their own code of conduct. After an unprecedented meeting in 1989 of all national editors, a declaration was issued stating, amongst other things:

> While supporting the Press Council, each individual newspaper now accepts the need to improve its own method of self-regulation, including procedures for dealing promptly and fairly with complaints. Editors have agreed on a Common Code of Practice and the establishment of systems of readers' representatives or ombudsmen, to take up complaints and breaches of the code.

The code of practice states:

- Intrusion into private lives should always have a public interest justification.
- A fair opportunity for reply will be given when reasonably called for.
- Mistakes will be corrected promptly and with appropriate prominence.
- Subject only to the existence of an overriding public interest, information for publication will be obtained by straightforward means.
- Newspapers will not authorise payment to criminals to enable them to profit from crime.
- Irrelevant reference to race, colour and religion will be avoided.

To the jaundiced eye, the code is as leaky as a sieve, but it does at least reflect the industry's awareness that, if it's to stop the government intervening, it has to be seen to be putting its house in order.

Complaints procedure – radio and television

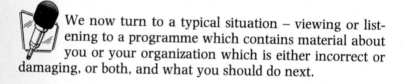 We now turn to a typical situation – viewing or listening to a programme which contains material about you or your organization which is either incorrect or damaging, or both, and what you should do next.

Getting your complaint aired

In its Television Programme Guidelines, the IBA states:

> corrections of factual errors should ... be broadcast as soon as is sensibly possible after the original error.

At the time of going to press, both BBC TV and Channel 4 (ITV) provided outlets for viewers' opinions.

Very early in its existence, Channel 4 introduced 'the video box', which allows anyone to record his or her point of view on video. Similar to a photographic booth, but without the disconcerting flash bulbs, in the video box all you have to do is look at a blank screen, press a button to activate the video camera and record your message. If you're not satisfied with your performance, you can re-record, but there are no editing facilities. Such has been the success of the video box that several have been established throughout the country. Contact Channel 4 (60 Charlotte Street, London W1P 2AX, telephone: 071–631 4444) for details.

Right to Reply (Channel 4), which sometimes broadcasts comments recorded in the video box, has been running since 1982. The programme offers viewers an opportunity to answer back those who make, commission or schedule television programmes. They can contribute to the programme by letter, telephone or the video box. Some will also have the opportunity to confront the programme-makers in the studio. Brian Hayes, the programme's presenter, says:

> I'm glad *Right to Reply* isn't the sort of programme which makes fun of the viewing community, but instead takes them seriously. When viewers think a programme has failed television's high standards, *Right to Reply* has a valuable role in helping them find out why.

Open Air (BBC) is a daily hour-long magazine programme about television, during which the general public is invited to express its views, either in person or by telephone. The programme tends to be more of an opinion piece than a forum for detailed complaints.

Network (BBC) appears monthly, and is part of the BBC Community Programmes Unit. It covers issues besides television, and gives people the right to make their own films in order to put their point of view across.

Points of View (BBC) consists of readings of extracts from viewers' letters, presented in a lighthearted style.

Most public access on radio is provided via the ubiquitous phone-in and the long-running Radio 4 programme *Any Ques-*

tions, which tends to deal with general, rather than specific, topics.

Formal complaints

In addition to attempting to get your complaint aired on television or radio, there is a well-worn path leading to possible redress:

1 Telephone the relevant television or radio company (there is always someone on duty) and lodge a complaint, making sure to keep a note of the time of your call, the contents of the conversation and the name of the recipient.
2 Telephone Tellex Monitors (see Chapter 1) and ask for a transcript and/or a video of the programme.
3 Contact the producer of the particular programme and follow up your complaint in writing, with a copy to the programme controller. Always make sure you write to a name rather than a title.
4 If you don't get anywhere with the producer, write a further letter to the programme controller, copying *all* the correspondence to the managing director.
5 At the risk of generating a great deal of paperwork, if you feel you're still not getting anywhere, also direct your complaint to the Independent Broadcasting Authority (or Independent Television Commission and Radio Authority, as it will become), the Director-General of the BBC (Michael Checkland) or the BBC's General Advisory Council.
6 If none of these avenues brings satisfaction, you should seriously consider taking up the matter with the Broadcasting Complaints Commission or the Broadcasting Standards Council.

Broadcasting Complaints Commission (Grosvenor Gardens House, 35–37 Grosvenor Gardens, London SW1B 0BS, telephone: 071–630 1966)

The Broadcasting Complaints Commission (BCC) is an independent body established in 1981, and is empowered to consider complaints of unjust or unfair treatment in radio, television or cable programmes actually broadcast, or unwarranted infringement of privacy in, or in connection with, some programmes. You may complain only if you were a participant in the programme, or if you have a direct interest in it. It's not enough simply to disagree with the treatment of a programme. Complaints regarding infringement of privacy must be made by the person whose privacy has been infringed. In exceptional circumstances, a complaint may be made on behalf of someone else with their permission, or on behalf of someone who has died. In the latter case, the complaint must be made within five years of the person's death.

The Commission *cannot* consider complaints about any of the following:

- the depiction of sex or violence (see Broadcasting Standards Council);
- bad language;
- any subject under the broad headings of 'taste', or 'standards';
- programme scheduling;
- a programme which is in the course of production or which has not yet been broadcast.

Complaints should be made in writing to The Secretary to the Commission, giving the programme title, time and date of transmission and relevant TV channel. It's important at this stage to give a full description of your complaint and to explain your direct interest.

On receipt of the complaint, the Commission will decide whether it falls within their jurisdiction or whether there are any other reasons why it can't consider it (for instance, it won't accept a complaint which is currently the subject of legal proceedings or which it considers frivolous).

Once a complaint has been accepted, however, copies are sent to the relevant broadcasting bodies, who must provide a transcript of the programme. If the Commission wishes, it can ask for a written statement and comments from the complainant. A hearing might then be arranged, at which the complainant and the broadcasting body may be asked to appear separately or together. The Commission's findings are set out in a written adjudication.

Copies of the adjudication are first sent to both parties. It's the Commission's normal practice, *whether or not the complaint has been upheld,* to direct the broadcasting body to broadcast the summary and to publish it in the *Radio Times* or *TV Times* as appropriate. The broadcast usually occurs at a similar time to when the original programme went out. The national and provincial press also receive the summary. The Commission cannot insist that the broadcasting body apologize to the complainant or broadcast a correction or provide financial recompense.

Here is an example of a recent BBC adjudication:

Wales Today BBC1 (Wales) – Complaint from 'The A–Z of Motoring' Summary of Adjudication (May 1989):

The Broadcasting Complaints Commission, who are concerned with fairness and privacy, have upheld a complaint about a news item broadcast on BBC–1 (Wales) on 8th March, 1989. This was the second of two items about court proceedings against two men who had tricked people into taking bogus driving tests. The first item described one of those men as the owner of 'The A–Z School of Motoring'. Mr Zapettis, the proprietor of the similarly named but entirely separate 'A–Z of Motoring', asked the BBC to announce that there was no connection between the two driving schools. The BBC refused the request, and broadcast the second item in which the 'A–Z School of Motoring' was again named without qualification.

The Commission consider that Mr Zapettis had clearly demonstrated after the first broadcast that there was a damaging possibility of confusion between the names of the two driving schools. In so far as the distinction was not made clear to the public in the second bulletin, the item was unfair and unjust to the complainant.

Broadcasting Standards Council (5–8 The Sanctuary, London SW1P 3JS, telephone (complaints staff): 071–233 0405)

Like the BCC, the Broadcasting Standards Council deals with complaints about all television and radio programmes. Again, though, it is empowered only to consider certain sorts of complaints.

Set up in 1988 on a non-statutory basis and chaired by Lord Rees-Mogg, its first task was to draw up a code of practice. The Council is concerned with the portrayal in programmes of violence and sexual conduct and with issues of taste and decency. Its 50-page code, which will be amended from time to time as attitudes change, gives detailed guidance to broadcasters on how these matters should be handled. The code is available, free of charge, from the Council's offices, to any interested members of the broadcasting audience.

The present Broadcasting Bill will confer statutory status on the Council, which will then be able to deal formally with complaints under a procedure to be announced later in 1990. Its findings will be made public.

Until that time, the Council welcomes comments and observations on programmes as a means of increasing its understanding of the public's views on what they are currently seeing and hearing.

Radio Authority (70 Brompton Road, London SW3 1EY, telephone: 071–584 7011)

All commercial radio, when the new Broadcasting Act comes into force, will come under the aegis of the newly established Radio Authority, to be chaired by Lord Chalfont, with Peter Baldwin as Chief Executive. The Radio Authority will be responsible for awarding the licences for the proposed national commercial stations.

Complaints procedure – the press

The Press Council* (1 Salisbury Square, London EC4Y 8AE, telephone: 071–353 1248).

Like its sister organizations in television and radio, the Press Council is changing. For the first time in its 37 years, a general code of practice – the first to cover all newspapers and magazines in Britain – was adopted in March 1990.

Until then the Council relied on building up precedent by its adjudications on individual complaints and declarations of principle on particular subjects instead of publishing a formal code. This code was adopted as part of the Press Council's review of its role and functions, and includes items on accuracy, opportunity to reply, intrusions into privacy and grief, comment and fact, journalist's use of subterfuge, chequebook journalism, interviewing and naming children, and press reference to race and colour.

The Press Council was founded in 1953. At present, there is no charge for its services and it is available to anyone who has a complaint to make against a British newspaper or periodical, whether or not they have a direct or personal interest in the matter about which they are complaining. One of its principal objectives is to deal with complaints in a practical and appropriate manner and to record resultant action.

It's important that a complaint is made *promptly*. A delay of more than a month is unacceptable unless there are special circumstances. A person making a complaint via the Press Council is expected to wait for adjudication before taking any alternative steps to seek redress, including any legal action. The Council does *not* deal with commercial matters and cannot be used to recover debts, or to seek financial compensation.

I would strongly recommend that any organization likely to have dealings with the press takes the precaution of getting hold of a free copy of the Press Council's leaflet *Guidance on Procedure for Complainants*.

---

*Probably to be replaced by an independent Press Complaints Commission.

Fast-track complaints

In 1984 the Press Council introduced a 'fast-track' complaints procedure, established to deal specifically with *factual* errors or inaccuracies. Your request for a correction must be submitted to the editor of the relevant publication, making clear that it is under Press Council Correction Procedure, with a copy of the request and of the item concerned to the Press Council. Complainants may suggest appropriate wording for a correction, but they are not bound to do so.

The editor must publish the correction within *three working days* of receiving your letter, and if this is not complied with, or you are not satisfied with the editor's reply, you must inform the Press Council which will make a ruling.

Other complaints

If your complaint doesn't come in the 'fast track' category, the procedure will take longer.

Full particulars of your complaint (including a copy of any relevant published material) should be sent to the Director of the Press Council (currently Kenneth Morgan, MBE). Your correspondence will be circulated and a copy forwarded to the editor without comment. This gives him time to take any action he thinks fit, and perhaps respond directly to you.

If you don't receive a response within *seven* days, or you are not satisfied with what is sent to you, you should write again to the Director of the Press Council, stating details of your complaint and what you thought was improper. Always send copies of letters sent and received and the published material about which you are complaining. Witnesses can also submit statements.

Your complaint may be considered in three ways:

● conciliation
● investigation
● oral hearing

CONCILIATION

Some complaints may be promptly remedied by the publication of a correction, an explanation or an apology. You can ask that your complaint be dealt with this way.

INVESTIGATION

If conciliation isn't tried, or fails, the Complaints Secretary and his staff will investigate on behalf of the Council by putting evidence to the editor for him to answer. A dossier of relevant evidence is compiled for the Complaints Committee, which consists of an equal number of press and public members. The Committee may:

- halt the inquiry if there is not a case to answer;
- call for further evidence, including oral, if necessary;
- recommend a finding to the Council;
- take other appropriate action.

ORAL HEARINGS

Oral hearings are informal, and both the complainant and the journalist/editor involved may speak. There is no legal representation at this stage, although a complainant may bring a friend to act as an adviser.

Adjudications

At the completion of all the necessary stages, the findings will be considered by the Council and any adjudication sent by post before being generally released.

If the Council finds in your favour, you can expect their adjudication to be published. Unfortunately, as we all know, a Press Council adjudication or apology is seldom given the same prominence as the original article.

The Press Council is a body concerned with ethics, not law, so if legal action has been threatened, or is considered a possibility, the Council will not adjudicate unless the complainant has signed a waiver. This is an agreement not to take legal action if the editor agrees to co-operate in the investigation and to publish the Council's adjudication.

Complaining via the courts

> Reputation, reputation, reputation! O, I have lost my reputation!
> (*Othello*, Act 2 Scene 3)

Suing newspapers can be *very expensive*. An action in 1989 in the High Court, in which Lord Aldington, a former Deputy Conservative Party Chairman, successfully sued the historian Count Nikolai Tolstoy, and property dealer Nigel Watts, over allegations that Lord Aldington was a war criminal, is thought to have incurred legal costs of over £1 million.

A partner in a city firm of solicitors is likely to charge about £175 an hour, an assistant solicitor about £125 an hour, and an articled clerk about £50 an hour. Counsel's brief could be anything up to £20,000, and there's usually a daily rate during the court action of between £1,000–£2,000, added to which are the costs of junior counsel. The length of time spent in court is anyone's guess.

If, however, you win your case and you have a sympathetic jury (most libel cases are still heard in front of a jury), damages can be very generous. For instance, despite the fact that the judge hearing the Aldington case had allegedly told the jury to keep its feet firmly on the ground when awarding damages, they broke all records by awarding the plaintiff £1.5 million. This was £1 million more than the damages paid to the author and playwright Jeffrey Archer, whose £500,000 libel award was estimated to have cost £700,000 in legal fees.

Law of defamation (England and Wales)

Libel is defamation published in a form to which some degree of permanence attaches – writing, printing, drawings, photo-

173

graphs and, since the Defamation Act 1952, radio and television.

Slander is defamation in transitory form, such as by use of speech or gesture.

There are important legal differences between libel and slander which, however, are unlikely to be relevant to claims against the media and are therefore ignored in this chapter.

Publication of a libel can result in:

- a civil action for damages, an apology and costs;
- an injunction to prevent repetition; and/or
- a criminal prosecution against those responsible.

CIVIL LIBEL CASES

Legal aid is not available for civil libel cases. They are usually heard by a judge and jury, with the judge determining whether the words complained of are capable of being defamatory, and the jury deciding whether they are defamatory of the plaintiff and the amount of any award. You don't have to prove that you've suffered any loss – the law presumes damage.

The main purpose of a libel claim is to compensate for injury to reputation and hurt to the plaintiff's feelings. Additional damages may be given if it appears that a defendant has behaved malevolently ('aggravated' damages), and more still if a defendant has published hoping that his economic gain will outweigh any damages he would have to pay ('exemplary' or 'punitive' damages). If the libel is trivial, damages may be 'nominal'.

In a civil libel case, the plaintiff must establish the following:

- That the matter complained of has been published by the defendant. In the legal sense, this means that the information has been communicated to a person other than the plaintiff, although the scope of publication can be taken into account by the jury in considering the amount of damages to be paid.
- That the matter refers to the plaintiff. A name is not necessarily needed here, merely proof that others reading/seeing/hearing the published matter would recognize it

as referring to the plaintiff. The test is not whether the writer/broadcaster intended to refer to this person.

- That the matter is defamatory (see above). Tests may be as follows:
  (i) Does the matter complained of tend to lower the plaintiff in the estimation of right-thinking members of society?
  (ii) Does it tend to bring the plaintiff into hatred, ridicule, contempt, dislike or disesteem with society?
  (iii) Does it tend to make the plaintiff shunned or avoided or cut off from society?
  (iv) Does it injure the plaintiff's reputation in his or her office, trade or profession?

An inaccurate claim does not necessarily involve liability. It is the adverse impact on *reputation* that matters.

There are a number of possible defences to a libel action, of which the principal ones are as follows:

Justification

English law does not protect the reputation that a person either does not or should not possess. Stating the truth, therefore, does not incur liability. However, it is for the defendant to prove that what he or she has published is true, not for the plaintiff to disprove it. And proof must be thorough. For example, to quote an instance of a person using bad language is not enough to prove that the person is 'foul-mouthed'.

It is also insufficient for the defendant to prove that he or she has accurately repeated what a third person has written or said.

Fair comment

'Fair', in this context, means 'honest', so 'fair comment' means a writer's genuinely held opinion on a matter of public interest. It may be an extreme opinion, but still 'fair'. However, this defence can only apply when what is complained of is comment as distinct from a statement of fact. To impute something about a person's moral character, especially if he or she is a private

175

individual, and in most cases when he or she is a public figure, generally exceeds the bounds of fair comment.

Privilege

Privilege is divided into 'absolute' and 'qualified'. Public interest requires that persons in certain positions, such as judges and Members of Parliament, should be permitted to express themselves with complete freedom. To secure this independence, absolute privilege is given to their acts and words. Therefore, no action lies against judges, counsel, jury and witnesses in court proceedings and most official tribunals. The same applies to proceedings in Parliament and local councils and also to official reports of their proceedings. Absolute privilege also applies in respect of advice given by ministers of the Crown to the state and in other analogous situations.

The defence of 'qualified' privilege affords protection on certain occasions to persons acting in good faith and without improper motive who make statements about another person which are in fact not true and are defamatory.

There is a wide set of circumstances where this can apply, but in general there must be a common and corresponding duty or interest between the person who makes the communication and the person who receives it. This defence can be rebutted where it is proved that the defendant was actuated by express malice.

An example of a situation where qualified privilege would apply is where an employer makes statements concerning an employee's character in a reference. Media reports of judicial and other proceedings and statements made at public bodies are also subject to the defence of qualified privilege.

Apology or offer of amends

Apology under the Libel Acts 1834 and 1845 is rarely used as it presumes guilt and can therefore get the defendant into hot water. However, if the conditions are fulfilled – malice was not intended and a full apology has been printed in a newspaper of the plaintiff's choice before the libel case began – then it is a defence, although a sum must still be paid in compensation.

More frequently an 'offer of amends' is made under the Defamation Act 1952, where an 'innocent' or unintentional defamation has occurred. The offer to publish an apology must be made promptly. If accepted, it is a bar to proceedings.

Limitation

The Limitation Acts prevent proceedings for defamation three years after publication, though exceptions may be made where the plaintiff did not know of the publication. However, subsequent publications of defamatory material mean that a new libel action can be launched.

CRIMINAL LIABILITY IN LIBEL AND RELATED AREAS

The object of action for criminal libel is to punish the wrongdoer by fine or imprisonment, rather than merely to compensate the person defamed. However, criminal proceedings should not be instituted unless the libel is calculated to provoke a breach of the peace; the person defamed should, as a rule, use civil remedies rather than criminal.

There are four types of writing which may provoke a prosecution:

- Defamatory libel – not usually in a criminal case, but there are exceptions to this rule.
- Obscene publications. The defence would be that the publication is justified as being for the public good, i.e, is in the interests of science, literature, art or learning.
- Sedition and incitement to racial hatred.
- Blasphemous libel – extremely offensive writing/broadcasting concerning the Christian faith.

So, a framework exists at many levels to allow you to seek justice. However, always be wary of your own indiscretions, or you may find that the roles are reversed. Remember the cardinal rule: don't attack your competitors.

A former Holy Roman Emperor, Ferdinand I, used to say:

Let justice be done, though the world perish.

I say:

Dealing with the media is like sex – it gets better with practice.

Remember

- Prevention is better than cure.
- Injunctions can buy time.
- Lodge your complaint immediately with the relevant television or radio station or publication.
- Follow up a verbal complaint by writing to the producer of a radio or television station or the editor of a publication.
- You can sometimes get your complaint aired on dedicated complaints programmes on television and radio.
- Keep copies of all the correspondence.
- If an apology or correction isn't forthcoming in television and radio, write to the Broadcasting Complaints Commission (copying it to the Independent Television Commission, the Radio Authority and, if appropriate, the Broadcasting Standards Council and the Director-General of the BBC).
- Press complaints should be directed to the Press Council.
- If you're going to pursue the matter through the courts, go to a specialist solicitor for advice.

Conclusion: courage

If the Creator had a purpose in equipping us with a neck, he surely meant us to stick it out.
Arthur Koestler, *Encounter*, 1970

It takes courage to take on the media.

But courage is a commodity anyone involved in business has in abundance.

Learn some of the techniques described in this book and, who knows, you and I might well meet across a microphone.

Glossary

Action   TV director's command to begin filming

Angle   Main focus of story

Audio   Sound

Auto-cue   Text of speech reflected on glass screens or small TV monitor below camera

Back-announcement   Closing remarks of an item

Back-credit   Recap of names of interviewees

By-line   Name of author of story or programme

Byte   Brief sound or visual extracts

Cans   Headphones

Cart machine   Equipment used to record and play very short sound items for frequent broadcast (e.g. commercials)

Chroma key   Electronic device which allows one image to be superimposed on another

Control room   Room facing sound booth in a radio studio, occupied by engineer and possibly a producer/director

Copy   Journalist's or reporter's text

C/U   Close-up

Cue   Director's instruction to activate either broadcaster or equipment

Cue script   Reporter's or presenter's introductory text

Cut   Director's instruction to 'stop', or edit point in an item

Cut-away   Alternative picture often used to link edited footage

Delay   Few seconds' time lag electronically inserted in live broadcasts to allow profanities to be deleted

Door-stepping   Uninvited journalists visiting your home or office

Down the line   Telephone lines of broadcast quality

Dubbing   Transferring or mixing audio and visuals

ENG   Electronic news gathering

Feed   Audio or visual input from external source

Flip chart   Large pad of paper usually mounted on stand

Footage   Film of an event

Gallery   TV control room, usually overlooking the studio

Grams   Record players

Green room   Place where guests resist temptation of alcohol while waiting to go into the studio

Hook   Main point of story

Insert   Separate item which forms part of longer programme

Intro   Introduction

IPS   Inches per second

Jingle   Short piece of music, sometimes with song

Level   Sound balance

Line-up   Either camera rehearsal or running order of items

Live   Broadcast as events occur, i.e. not recorded

L-S   Long shot

Master   Original recording

Menu   Sequence of items in programme

Monitor   Small TV screen used to display live action or information to presenters or control room staff

M-S   Mid-shot

Music bed   Usually refers to music to be used as background to the voice-over in a commercial or programme

Noddies   Usually mute shots of reporter looking interested, recorded at end of interview

OB unit   Outside broadcast unit

Off-line editing   Preliminary film edit

Off the record   Journalists' trick to gain your confidence

On-line editing   Final film edit

Overheads   A visual aid projecting image drawn on acetate

Pan   Slow movement of camera from side to side

Peg   Key point of story – same as hook

Phone-in   Programmes in which viewers or listeners can talk to presenter and guests

Pre-record   Record an item for later broadcast

Profanity button   Activates 'delay' system to delete expletives

Radio car   Mobile sound broadcasting unit

Raw stock   Virgin audio or video tape

Read-through   Rehearsal

Reel-to-reel   Magnetic tape used for recording sound

Release form   Document you might be asked to sign releasing your interview for use as a programme thinks fit

Reverses   A reporter's repeated questions used in film editing – similar to noddies

Running order   Sequence of items in a programme

Run-through   Rehearsal

Scoop   Story exclusive to one paper or TV/radio station

Self-op   Control and sound booths combined, self-operated by disc jockey/presenter

SFX   Sound effects

Sting   Very short piece of music (jingle)

Subs   Editorial press team responsible for correcting copy and writing headlines

Syndication   Distribution of an interview around the UK/world

Talk-back   Link between control room and studio

Talking heads   Group discussion

Tele-cine   Film inserts

Transcript   Written presentation of speech

Two-way   Interview between two people

VCR   Video cassette recorder

VHS   Video Home Standard

Vox pop   Edited sequence of very brief interviews with members of the public

VTR   Video tape-recorder

White balance   A method of ensuring video camera's accurate colour reproduction

Wide shot   Group shot

Wrap   Director's instruction to shut up shop and repair to nearest pub

Zoom lens   Enables camera to move from a wide shot to a close-up without losing focus

Bibliography

Atkinson, Max, *Our Masters' Voices* (Methuen, 1984).

Bland, Michael and Simon Mondesir, *Promoting Yourself on Television and Radio* (Kogan Page, 1987).

Blue Book of British Broadcasting (Tellex Monitors, annual).

Day, Robin, *Sir Robin Day – Grand Inquisitor* (Weidenfeld and Nicolson, 1989).

Green, Jonathan (ed.), *Pan Dictionary of Contemporary Quotations* (Pan, 1989).

Hannaford, Peter, *Talking Back to the Media* (Facts on File, USA, 1986).

Hilton, Jack, *How to Meet the Press – A Survival Guide* (Dodd Mead, USA, 1987).

Lewis, Dr David, *The Secret Language of Success* (Bantam, 1989).

Lancaster, Graham, *The 20% Factor – The Key to Personal and Corporate Success* (David and Charles, 1987).

McCallion, Michael, *The Voice Book* (Faber and Faber, 1988).

Morris, Desmond, *Manwatching – A Field Guide to Human Behaviour* (Triad Panther, 1985).

Ross Boynton, Phil, *Winning the Media Game* (Stoddart, USA, 1989).

Saunders, James, *Nightmare – The Ernest Saunders Story* (Hutchinson, 1989).

Schmertz, Herb and William Novak, *Goodbye to the Low Profile – The Art of Creative Confrontation* (Mercury, USA, 1986).

Sharpe, Robert and Dr David Lewis, *The Anxiety Antidote* (Souvenir, 1979).

Writers' and Artists' Yearbook (A. & C. Black, annual).

Useful addresses and telephone numbers

Advance, Theme Tree Ltd, 2 Prebendar Court, Oxford Road, Aylesbury, Bucks HP 19 3EY (0296 28585)

BBC Television Centre, Wood Lane, London W12 7RJ (081–743–8000)

BBC Radio, Broadcasting House, London W1A 1AA (071–580 4468)

The British Library Newspaper Section, Colindale Avenue, London NW9 5HE (071–636 1544)

British Satellite Broadcasting (BSB), Marco Polo Building, Chelsea Bridge, Queenstown Road, London SW8 4NQ (071–978 2222)

The Broadcasting Complaints Commission, Grosvenor Gdns House, 35 Grosvenor Gdns, London SW1W 0BS (071–630 1966)

The Broadcasting Standards Council, 5–8 The Sanctuary, London SW1P 3JS (071–233–0544)

Channel Four, 60 Charlotte Street, London W1P 2AX (071–631–4444)

Electric Airwaves (Media Training Consultants), Essel House, 29 Foley St, London W1P 7LB (071–323 2770)

Independent Broadcasting Authority (IBA), 70 Brompton Road, London SW3 1EY (071–584–7011)

Ladbroke Radio Productions (Independent Radio Production House), Essel House, 29 Foley St, London W1P 7LB (071–323–2770)

The Law Society, 113 Chancery Lane, London WC2A 1PL (071–242–1222)

PIMS, 4 St John's Place, London EC1M 4AH (071–250–0870)

PNA Services Ltd, 13 Curtain Road, London EC2A 3LS (071–377–2521)

The Press Association, 85 Fleet St, London EC4P 4BE (071–353–7440)

The Press Council, 1 Salisbury Square, London EC4Y 8AE (071–353–1248)

Reuters, 85 Fleet St, London EC4P 4AJ (071–250 1122)

Romeike and Curtice, Hale House, Green Lane, London N13 5TP (081–882–0155)

Sky Television, 6 Centaur's Business Park, Grant Way, off Syon Lane,

Isleworth, Middlesex TW7 5QD (071–782–3000)
Tellex Monitors, 47 Gray's Inn Rd, London WC1X 8PR (071–405 7151)
Universal News Service (UNS), Communications House, Gough Square,
London EC4P 4DP (071–353 5200)

Index

187

191